IT'S ALL GONNA BE OKAY

FROM MAD & SAD TO CALM & CONFIDENT

Kim Sunderland

FriesenPress

One Printers Way
Altona, MB R0G 0B0
Canada

www.friesenpress.com

Copyright © 2024 by Kim Sunderland
First Edition — 2024

All rights reserved.

No part of this publication may be reproduced in any form, or by any means, electronic or mechanical, including photocopying, recording, or any information browsing, storage, or retrieval system, without permission in writing from FriesenPress.

ISBN
978-1-03-919041-2 (Hardcover)
978-1-03-919040-5 (Paperback)
978-1-03-919042-9 (eBook)
978-1-03-919043-6 (Audiobook)

1. SELF-HELP / PERSONAL GROWTH / HAPPINESS
2. SELF-HELP / EMOTIONS
3. SELF-HELP / SELF-MANAGEMENT / STRESS MANAGEMENT

Distributed to the trade by The Ingram Book Company

The information and strategies included in this book are not meant to substitute the advice of your family physician or any other trained healthcare professional. You are advised to consult with a healthcare professional with regard to all matters pertaining to you and your family's health and well-being.

Table of Contents

PREFACE: THE VALUE OF A BATHROOM BOOK	IX
INTRODUCTION: WHAT TO EXPECT FROM THIS BOOK	XI
SECTION 1: LIFE IS INTERESTING	1
A Bit About Me	3
We Are All Finding Our Own Way	7
Who's Driving Your Car? Emotion or Logic?	11
Is It Possible to Find a New Way?	15
Angry Meltdowns and Toboggan Hills	16
Neurology—Kim Style	19
Finding Peaceful Calm and Appreciated Joy	23
SECTION 2: THANKFULLY, CHANGE HAPPENS	27
Leaning Toward the Hope for Something Better	29
I'm Not Part of the Problem, Am I?	31
Dr. P's Stages of Change	33
Supporting Others	37
The Next Moment, and Then the Next One After That	39
Running Away from Home—Adult Style	43
Finding a Supporter	45
Reach for What Works for YOU—Books and Audiobooks	47
What Might Help Through the Remainder of the Change Process	53
Adjusting Your Mindset	55
Oops!	57
Falling off the Wagon	59
Overcoming Reflexive Thoughts	63

SECTION 3: LEARNING MY WAY THROUGH LIFE — 67

   Stepping Stones — 69
   Parenting Classes—Doing It My Way! — 73
   Giving the Goofy Stuff a Try — 77
   Listening to Your Body — 81
   What's It Like to Do Psychotherapy? — 85
   Finding the Right Therapist for You — 89
   Exploring Your Deep-Down Beliefs — 91
   Throwing out the Rule Book — 95
   What Do I *Really* Want? — 99
   This Little Light of Mine — 103
   Life Is Like a Golf Shot—Envision It to Be Great — 107
   You Get What You Expect — 111
   Stop Arguing for Your Limitations — 115
   Pink-Chair Musings — 119
   Looking at Meds — 123
   Self-Care—Bring It On — 127
   The Mindset / Change Relationship — 131

SECTION 4: GROW YOUR RESILIENCE—IT'S ALREADY HAPPENING — 135

   Learning from My Resilience Tree — 137
   What the Experts Say — 141
   It Happened! Not Sure When or How, but It Happened! — 145
   To Dramatize or Not to Dramatize—That Is the Question — 149
   Life Is an Interconnected ~~Mess~~ Creation — 153
   Know Thyself—The Value of Self-Awareness — 157
   Contemplation as a Sleep Aid — 161
   Grounding Yourself in the Present Moment — 165
   Mindfully Growing Your Resilience — 169
   Meditation—Kim Style — 173
   It's in the Palm of Your Hands — 177
   There's More than One Way to Live Life — 181
   How Much "Practice" Does It Take? — 183

SECTION 5: BRINGING IT HOME—FORWARD WE GO   187

    Getting Ready to Be Ready to Be Ready . . .   189
    Yucky Days Still Happen   193
    Understanding Our Long-Ago Bruises   197
    A Lifetime of Unintentional Visualizations   199
    I Can Only Be Me   203
    Getting Comfortable with the DEL Key   207
    Becoming the New You   211
    Transitions Can Be Hard   215
    So Where Is My Cob of Corn?   219
    Getting Past the Challenges   223
    It's All Gonna Be Okay   227

ABOUT THE AUTHOR   229

PREFACE
The Value of a Bathroom Book

There was a time years ago when I did not have the time (or did not allow myself the time) to read a chapter of a book, let alone a whole book. Life felt too busy, I was too stressed, and "hard-working productive (good) people" like me did not selfishly waste time on things like reading. (*Yes, today I can hear the overwhelming judgment in those statements, but back then was a different time for me.*) This may feel familiar to you. For me, this is what it felt like to live with anxiety. I was overwhelmed all the time—in a big way—for a lot of reasons—and all of it seemed to be justified!

I do not recall how it happened, but I somehow acquired a little book called *Don't Sweat the Small Stuff, and It's All Small Stuff*, by Richard Carlson. The title appealed to me . . . I needed this. That book became the first of many self-help books, and it changed my life. Trust me, it took more than one book to "change my life," but it got me started on that journey.

That book became my bathroom book—meaning that I kept it in the bathroom and only allowed myself the time to read one, maybe two, pages at a time. That was perfect as each chapter was at most two pages, and each chapter was a story-based lesson.

Some of the lessons of that book are still highlights in my memory today. Reading that book helped me begin to realize that I could make changes to how I think, which kicked off a series of impacts. I discovered that what I *think* impacts how I *feel*, which impacts how I *live* day to day, which impacts my *happiness and satisfaction* with life, which impacts my *resiliency*, which impacts my true ability to be the *kind, patient, loving* person I have always tried to be.

As the years have gone by, I have found myself scribbling notes to myself about how I would share specific ideas that I have found helpful if I were to ever write a book. I have found several of my stories and ways of thinking to be helpful to others in my role as a mental health workshop facilitator. And I've often thought about that first "bathroom book" I read. That format makes so much sense to me, so I am now taking the plunge and writing my own bathroom book with short, easy-to-digest mini-chapters.

Each one of us humans is unique, and we, therefore, have an infinite number of approaches to overcoming difficulties and achieving a sense of calm and happiness. I remember what it was like when I knew I needed something to make life better, but every time I read something, it seemed like it was another item to be added to the to-do list. Work, kids, extracurriculars, parents, house, meals, groceries, and now I need to become less judgmental, exercise, walk in nature, and meditate in order to manage my mental wellness and grow my resilience! *Ya, sure, I'll get right on that!!* Not only is it on the to-do list, but it's also on that other list: things to feel guilty about. *What happens if I do not become resilient? Will I break? Am I already broken? This is not what I expected. I thought I was going to be "perfect." Maybe I'm a perfectionist. Oh no!! Something else to add to the to-do list—become perfect without being a perfectionist.*

If you feel like you cannot calm your mind (or life) enough to try out some recommended wellness activities—heck, you can't even calm your mind enough to sleep through the night—then this book is for you.

INTRODUCTION
What to Expect from This Book

I won't prescribe a wellness journey for you, but I'll lay out some of my favourite "feel-better strategies" that you can try, like stepping stones. Better yet, I'll encourage you to come up with your own strategies and next steps.

As someone who champions peer support, I believe it isn't my role to tell you what you *should* be doing. Your mental wellness path is unique to you. You will know instinctually what you would like to try and which strategy is best for you. I'm here to offer my experience as someone who has been in that yucky place, found my way out, and been blessed to continue learning through my work in this field.

Over the last decade, I have built a career as a mental health educator and peer support workshop facilitator. This has allowed me to learn more about the science and best practices that back up the theories and approaches that naturally made sense to me as I tried to find my way to a happier place.

Key components of peer support include hope, self-determination, and empowerment. Transferring the meaning of self-determination—that the person themselves has the answer to what is best for them within themselves—to a personal level helped to reinforce my long-held belief that I had the inner wisdom to know what was right for me as I strived forward on my wellness journey.

Having a non-judgmental approach to all whom we strive to support is another peer support principle. Again, there is wisdom in applying this on a personal level. How helpful is it to be constantly judging ourselves and finding ourselves to be stupid, lazy, or not good enough? Kindness and compassion for ourselves is the opposite of self-judgment—and for me, it allowed a huge leap forward.

Over time, by practising wellness techniques, you will find you can make changes to your self-talk and your mindset. Your mindset is the way you view the world and/or interpret what happens around you. In other words, do you interpret a lot of what you experience as intentional disrespect from others and/or do you believe you experience more than your fair share of bad luck? (This way of thinking may be an indicator of an unhappy or blaming mindset.)

Or do you view those unfortunate happenings as hiccups that are barely worth noticing, as there are so many other gratifying things in your world? (This would be an example of an *extraordinarily* positive mindset!) Most of us fall somewhere between these two endpoints.

Working on adjustments to your self-talk and mindset will, in turn, help you to feel more in control of your emotions. Even better, all of this leads you toward developing greater resiliency. All the little things I've included in this book that helped me to feel better in the moment were, in fact, also part of my resiliency practice—even though I didn't know it at the time. And the work I did in years gone by continues to pay off today when those bad moments want to once again rear their ugly little heads.

It's All Gonna Be Okay begins with a discussion of the impact of emotions and my toboggan hill theory in the first section, as it underpins much of what follows. Section 2 is all about change and the stages that we all pass through as we strive to adjust whatever it is that is causing us pain. "Learning Forward" and "Stepping Stones" (Section 3) share a wide range of coping strategies and ways of thinking that can support us through the hard days and/or encourage the personal growth that we desire. Resiliency (Section 4) is what it's all about. In many cases, resiliency is an overused word, but you will hopefully share my opinion that each time we find a healthy way to cope, it is like we are putting another pebble on our path to resiliency growth. And finally, I "Bring It Home" in Section 5 with a look at how life continues forward as we also continue forward by *leaning in* toward a journey of personal growth and resiliency.

I hope you find this book to be both lighthearted and reassuring. The more we *should* on ourselves, the more we are keeping ourselves in a negative state of mind, so it only makes sense to take a light-hearted approach. And you *are* going to be okay. We both know deep in our souls that life can be gratifying and fun. The answers are there. It just gets hard trying to find those answers some days. *Stick with me. You've got this. It's all gonna be okay.*

SECTION 1
Life Is Interesting

A Bit About Me

I am blessed. I always have been. I have a roof over my head, food in my fridge, love in my life, a meaningful career, a family to care for, and friends to have fun with. I am most definitely blessed.

Alongside this, I have also had sleepless nights, non-stop tears of anger and misery, debilitating headache pain that would stay with me for days, and embarrassing and misguided fits of verbal abuse toward whoever was nearby—and thankfully, years of psychotherapy with a kind and supportive therapist.

So, who am I, really? It's complicated. Our self-image is complicated. At least mine is.

Am I, in fact, the kind, confident, capable, and patient person many have seen for most of my life? Or am I the mad and sad person I have experienced for some of the more painful private times of my life?

These days, I hardly ever feel the extreme *mad* or *sad* that I recall experiencing in days gone by. And when I do feel it coming, I can usually help myself ward it off. It's been a journey—a journey of the most important kind.

I'm telling you this in the hopes that my honesty helps you relate and feel hopeful that we—you and me—really are good people. The people we wish to be. And that we can shrink, to almost nothingness, the mad and sad parts of us.

I've given up trying to figure out why. Yes, there is a diagnosis of anxiety and depression, but why do I have that? Who knows? The bottom line is that, for me, in my journey, it doesn't matter why. What matters to me is how to get through the yucky times and come out on the other side feeling good to go. That's what this book is about.

I feel like I have managed to change my mindset. Or, rather, I feel like I have changed all the little mindsets that make up my overall approach to life. And with each little adjustment, I felt like it was a step in the right direction—of becoming more fully the person I was meant to be.

As I look back and recall the various thoughts, concepts, visualizations, and stories that were a part of that journey, I can see how they impacted my day-to-day life and, in particular, my resiliency. I think of my resiliency as my ability to remain hopeful and able to believe that life is working out and everything is going to be okay instead of thinking that life is going nowhere, or worse, downhill fast.

> Why write a book?
>
> *"Don't die with your story still in you."*
> WAYNE DYER
>
> I heard Wayne say this years ago in one of his audiobooks. At the time, it didn't resonate with me, but years pass, and life changes. Lately, this pops into my mind every now and then. Of course, my first thought is, *Who am I to write a book?* But then, I shift my thoughts and think, *Wouldn't it be a shame if I died with something more that I could offer—still inside of me—left undone?*
>
> So here I go!

This is not my "story." Rather, it is my attempt to share the more private aspects of my life. The parts that have caused me to face some of my biggest challenges and the "way of thinking" that I adopted in order to get through it. In other words, it is what works for me, and if it works for you, then I'm happy to offer it to you.

My hope is that my thoughts will stir your own inner thoughts, and you, too, will come up with your own way of thinking. It may be similar to mine or completely different. All that matters is that it is helpful for you. I look forward to reading your book one day.

If you're hearing me in your heart, then stick with me. I'm sending kindness and appreciation your way. Let's get this started! It's all gonna be okay.

We Are All Finding Our Own Way

There was a time when I was angry all the time. At least, it feels like that in my memory.

I was not the person who was shouting it from the rooftops—or across social media—but, unfortunately, I was angry and frustrated too often at home—with those I love the most. Or I was impatient and irritated with strangers I came across in daily life, such as customer service reps in stores or on phone calls. Yes, unfortunately, I was one of *those* people more often than I care to admit.

Thankfully, my husband tells me he doesn't remember it that way. Thank God for selective memory. But I do. And that is not, was not, who I wanted to be. In reality, it was not *all* the time, and it probably wasn't as bad as it is in my memory, but it was disruptive enough for me that it felt that way.

I am also very aware that I was able to hold it together more often than not and keep my emotions tied up inside. But that negative vibe inside me was hard to live with. Feeling like I was (somewhat) succeeding at keeping myself from expressing emotions such as mad and sad is not an ideal way to live.

In hindsight, I am now able to think of it as **emotional reactions** that were the problem. These reactions occurred almost instantaneously, to the point where I could not tell that my emotions had taken over, or that logic had left me, and I was acting out because I was feeling unappreciated—or feeling like precious time was being wasted—or feeling frustrated because other people were not agreeing with what seemed obvious to me—or any other of the various feelings that were common for me in those days.

Of course, it's much more complex than the few simple statements above, but the key is that logic left me, frustration or anger set in, and my mouth reacted by saying things I typically would not want to say. Or sadness would be the emotion that would set in, and hours of fearful, painful, lonely crying would result. Most likely, in these scenarios, if it started with anger, it would be closely followed by guilt (that I had let the anger out), fear (that I was driving people away from me), and sadness (that I was not able to keep it together and be the person I wanted to be). Oh, the joys of life?!

Emotions are interesting. For the first part of my life, I thought they could be put in boxes marked "good" and "bad." It was simple. If you had one of the bad emotions, then you were either not grateful enough because there were others in worse shape than you, or you were weak because you let things like fear and anger come to the forefront. Obviously, those statements are erroneous and shame-based, but at the time, those were my beliefs.

As a mental health workshop facilitator, I began to lead in-depth discussions about emotions. I know you are possibly thinking that is odd since I have just admitted to being oblivious to their true purpose and impact, but over time, I (finally) learned the wisdom of becoming more aware of what we are feeling.

The takeaway here is that there are no good or bad emotions. All emotions are natural—they are a part of being human.

There are definitely some emotions that are more pleasant to feel than others—that is for sure. But we cannot simply label them as good or bad. They all occur naturally, on a spectrum, and we are bound to experience that entire spectrum in our lifetime. It's what we do with the mad or sad or fearful emotion that is more important.

If we feel like we've just been insulted or slighted, then we might feel something in the anger category of emotions—that would be normal. Or if we have just lost a friend or a pet or our favourite pen, then we would feel something in the sad category. And fear-based emotions might arise if our (physical, emotional, or economic) safety feels threatened.

Of course, there is a full range of emotions beyond the anger, sad, and fear categories that I mention above. Look up "emotion wheel" to view an excellent resource outlining the range of emotions. And there is a continuum of how deeply we may feel an emotion. For example, the degree of sadness you would feel losing your favourite pen is different than the sadness felt when you lose a loved one.

If we are more aware of the cocktail of emotions we are feeling, then we are more likely to be able to decide what we want to do with those feelings when they occur. For example, in some cases, it might be wise to attempt to manage emotional turmoil by talking to another person. Or, in a different situation, it might be most respectful to ourselves to allow the mix of emotions to exist and sit with them for a while, recognizing that something significant is making us have all kinds of uncomfortable feelings—and that is okay.

> "If we are more aware of the cocktail of emotions we are feeling, then we are more likely to be able to decide what we want to do with those feelings when they occur."

It's when we are oblivious to our feelings or emotions (not aware that they are impacting us) that we end up reacting with very little thought about it.

Who's Driving Your Car? Emotion or Logic?

So, the bottom line: emotions are okay. We feel a wide variety of feelings, and that's the way life is. But *reactions* to our emotions are more risky and can possibly result in us reacting in a way we didn't plan.

The challenge is that it's often hard to tell the difference between the emotion and the reaction, or to recognize the pattern that an emotion (or, more likely, a complex series of emotions) is occurring and there will be a tendency to react. In other words, it can be challenging to realize that the steam is building and might soon blow!

Brené Brown, who is another inspiring author, describes this phenomenon as emotion being at the wheel of the car, with logical thought and behaviour not even in the back seat, but rather trapped in the trunk. Can you relate? Are you someone who (unfortunately)  remembers a time when you reacted with loud anger, self-centred tears, and/or fearful defensiveness, or worse? People like you and me are generally logical people who would never advise another person to react that way. But it happens. Sometimes, we find ourselves in the grip of emotional turmoil and not responding in the logical way we would expect of ourselves.

For me, the emotional reactions that are most prominent in my memory (because they bothered me the most) include screaming at my kids because they wouldn't stop arguing with each other (which means I was then demonstrating the very behaviour I wanted to stop); or verbally lambasting a spa receptionist because they didn't have appointments for me and my friends (I truly regret that day); or crying uncontrollably for hours after feeling unappreciated or unfairly treated by another person (I regret to say I have been that person more times than I wish to remember).

In the moment, I always felt justified. It was *not* my fault. It was those damn customer service people who could never give me what I wanted or the stupidity of business associates, school principals, or other drivers on the road. And try to get your kids to do anything when you are in a rush to get out the door. No, it was *never* my fault—I could not be blamed for exploding.

Often, when I was at home with my kids, I was smart enough to stomp up the stairs, yelling behind me that I was taking myself to my room and being somewhat pleased that I was role-modelling a self-imposed timeout. I would then pace around in my room, battling between feeling shame for poor behaviour and a righteous self-indignation for my being in the right—*what else could be expected of me?*

I had grown up to believe that it was "bad" to be mad, as in it was shameful misbehaviour to feel the angry/mad emotion. I concluded that those who (verbally) acted out on their anger were not behaving in an appropriate manner because they were feeling angry, not that it was their reaction to the emotion that was unfortunate. Since I didn't understand the difference between an emotion and an emotional reaction, my logic was that it was because people felt angry that they *behaved* in such a way. Therefore, I never described myself as angry or mad. Instead, I insisted I was frustrated. Frustration seemed to be a more allowable emotion. But I was too often really, really, really frustrated—and loud about it.

I'm wondering if you can relate to this, to times in your life when you were someone who blew up in anger. If that is not you, then you might be judging me pretty hard right now.

On the other hand, maybe you can't relate because you have an iron-clad defence—a justification for why you couldn't expect yourself to respond in any other way. Yep . . . been there, too. It's always the other person's fault, right? I cannot possibly agree or disagree with you on this one. Life is too complex, and each of us is unique in our life experiences. You may be right.

For me, it was a learning curve to realize that emotional reactions (outbursts or meltdowns) are related to my inner experiences and emotional habits. And while we all (supposedly) have control over what we *choose* to say and do in response to difficult situations, it's not that straightforward. It's not easy, or even possible sometimes, to simply force ourselves to *choose* to respond from a place of calm and control. That ability to *decide how to react* is a learning curve that takes time to become aware of, and it takes ongoing work to master it.

> "The way to start changing your mind is not to force it or command it, but to watch it."
>
> MARTHA BECK

Is It Possible to Find a New Way?

So now what? One option is to continue to react when emotions get triggered—which is what many of us tend to do if we have not yet found any other options. I obviously did not like it when I emotionally exploded. It never truly solved anything. Instead, it caused a whole new collection of uncomfortable feelings—in both myself and others.

My logical solution to emotional explosions in the early years was to promise myself that I would *never* do that again—promise myself that I would be a better, nicer, calmer person in the future who *never* emotionally explodes—for any reason. *Ya right!! Good luck with that.*

I tried over and over again, but I couldn't manage to catch myself when an emotional outburst was about to happen, or harder yet, turn it off as soon as it began. Instead, with each failed attempt at trying to stop myself from exploding, I became increasingly more defensive in justifying the reaction—and I felt even more awful about myself. There must be other choices.

For you, it might not be emotional explosions that are most prominent in your emotional life. Possibly, for you, it feels like emotional implosions or meltdowns instead? Whatever it might be that causes you to feel regret, that is what I am talking about. If you have no regrets about your emotional impulses, you may be skipping a few pages.

Angry Meltdowns and Toboggan Hills

I don't fully recall when or how this visualization actually came about, but I managed to create another option for myself. I remember sitting and thinking about all the above, probably after I had just blown up again and was (once again) chastising myself for being a terrible person who couldn't control herself even though I knew I should.

I started to visualize all this emotional turmoil as if I were on a toboggan, speeding along a slick, icy path down a big hill. There have been so many runs down this steep path, and it is now so slippery and icy that there is no chance of stopping or even slowing down—instead, the toboggan is gaining speed as it goes.

At the top of that hill, at the very edge of the slope, it seems like it only takes one more small nudge to get the toboggan on the downward slope, zipping down that hill so fast there won't be any time to think about what is happening—until it eventually comes to a standstill out in the middle of the flat field below.

More than once, I recall feeling like I had just slowed to a stop out in that field and was beginning to realize that I had done it again! I had let my mouth say all kinds of mean things, non-stop, at top volume. I had unconsciously allowed myself to zip down that slick toboggan path. I had not meant to say and do what I did, but once the sled got nudged over the edge, there was no holding me back. Ugh! What a terrible feeling.

Eventually, over time, I started to notice that it was happening again while in the middle of the emotional outburst. I noticed that I was *doing it*, but I just couldn't get myself together enough to stop.

As my awareness of these outbursts grew, I began trying to switch my inner dialogue. Instead of chastising myself, I would try to acknowledge and possibly even congratulate myself for noticing it was happening and think of it as some sort of progress. (Of course, I would keep all of this only in my thoughts because if I dared to share out loud that I was attempting to be proud of myself for becoming more aware, there was likely no one around who would cheer me on for noticing that it was happening, yet appear to let it continue happening.)

In addition to being (somewhat) pleased that I was becoming more self-aware, I would also visualize myself noticing it earlier, farther up the hill (earlier in my outburst), and I would encourage myself to find a way to get off that path earlier—to take a different path down the hill—in order to stop the outburst of anger.

Have you ever tried to veer off a well-worn toboggan path? Trying so hard to steer off the ice and into fresh snow alongside that has yet to be worn down by other toboggans. Whoa! That takes a *lot* of determination. You really have to lean into it. But it's possible! Even if you've only accomplished it once, that makes it possible.

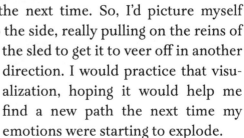

I'd consider this when sitting on my own (usually after yet *another* blow-up) and decide I truly wanted to get off that slick, dangerous, emotional explosion path the next time. So, I'd picture myself leaning as hard as I could to the side, really pulling on the reins of the sled to get it to veer off in another direction. I would practice that visualization, hoping it would help me find a new path the next time my emotions were starting to explode.

> "The good news is that if a new path has been attempted even once, then it becomes an alternate path, there for the taking the next time."

The good news is that if a new path has been attempted even once, then it becomes an alternate path, there for the taking the next time. I knew it still wouldn't be easy to make that turn—reality was demonstrating that to me. But I also knew that if I managed to lean into it and veer off onto that new path just a few times, the snow would get flattened down a bit more, and that off-ramp would be in existence and a bit easier to find in the future.

Hmmm. I continued to consider, *If I can turn off the path at that midway point, I wonder if I can turn off sooner—right after starting down the hill? No need to go halfway down and then veer off. Why can't I do it right after the start of the descent? And then, if I can do that, could I get good enough at noticing what was happening that I could maybe avoid the edge of the hill altogether?*

If you are not a visual person, this may seem a little odd to you, but for me, it was helpful.

The other thing I found to be extraordinarily helpful was to be intentional about being as kind as possible to myself after an outburst. I still held myself accountable when I acted in a way that I didn't like, but I also tried to think of myself in a kind and compassionate manner and keep faith in myself that I would eventually figure out how to react differently. Of course, I was not always successful at this. Most often, my first reaction after calming down would be to berate myself for behaving so badly. But then, after a period of time, I would at least try to turn it around and show myself some compassion. Somehow, I knew that was important.

Neurology–Kim Style

I'm not sure which came first, reading the book *The Brain That Changes Itself*, by Norman Doidge, or visualizing my toboggan hill. I think they both came to me at around the same time.

If you thought the toboggan hill concept was a little too offbeat, you might be skeptical about this upcoming biology lesson on neurology. But I'm going to go for it anyway.

We now know that the brain is not hard-wired and can rewire itself over time. Decades ago, they thought the various sections of the brain were static. If you lost one part of your brain to something like a stroke or traumatic injury, then the tasks associated with that part of the brain could not be regained. Doidge tells several stories of people regaining their ability to walk or talk, for example. What makes this cool is that when they do brain scans, you can actually see where a different part of the brain has rewired to support relearning these functions.

In other words, there is space in the brain for the development of new skills (or, alternatively, to adjust old skills, habits, or emotional reactions). If the *walking skill* part of the brain is still functional, then it will always stay there. But if you lose that part of the brain and, therefore, lose your ability to walk, it might be possible to relearn all the individual stages of learning to walk so the brain could rewire it into another area. (Like I said, I am *not* a scientist. I have extensively paraphrased and oversimplified, but the bottom line is that if one person can find a way to rewire their brain, then we can say that it is now considered a possibility.)

As I listened to this audiobook years ago, I spent a lot of time thinking about how the synapses and myelination and all the other cool "brain stuff" worked together to allow this to happen. I could visualize that if I were to begin learning how to play the piano, my brain would not yet be proficient at helping me figure out where to put my fingers on the keyboard. But if I continued to practice, the synapses in my brain would start to fuse together. Eventually, after years of practice, I would have some well-worn paths throughout my brain that get put to use every time I sit down at a piano. Kind of reminds me of a well-worn, super slick toboggan hill after going down the path a few dozen times. Hmmmm.

> "Neurons that fire together, wire together."
>
> DONALD HEBB

If my brain lays down well-worn paths for all the other repetitive things I do—like walk, talk, and hit a golf ball—then it only stands to reason that there would be some well-worn paths up there related to my emotions and, more importantly, my emotional reactions. That would include my positive reactions—like when I instinctively offer a hug to someone who feels sad—as well as my less favourable reactions, like when I get angry at someone who I feel has slighted me in some manner.

This may not be biologically accurate, but my visualization is that there are a zillion well-worn paths up there in my brain with actions and reactions happening all over the place. And unfortunately, some of those are like the toboggan hill of negative reaction that I am trying to dismantle.

My personal conclusion is if it is possible for a person to walk and talk again after a major trauma such as a stroke, then it is biologically possible (not easy, but possible) for each of us to think about modifying some of the unwanted emotional reactions that we are aware of, and not fond of. Why not? It might take a bit of time, but it can and will happen.

At the time, it all felt like one big mess of a problem, but now, when I look back, I can see that several things were happening at the same time. In part, I was dismantling the emotional reactions—not just the explosions and implosions, but also the smaller emotional reactions that would happen within my body and my thoughts. It can eliminate a lot of extra pain to be less *stormy* when around others, but it is also no fun to live with the dark clouds on the inside.

I wanted to be able to go through life with less emotional effort. I wanted to feel more of the easy-going and fun emotions on a daily basis, rather than just be successful at keeping the dark emotions from exploding out. At the time, that felt like I needed to learn how to cope better with what life threw at me.

Finding Peaceful Calm and Appreciated Joy

Great! Get me some of that! Who wouldn't want peaceful calm and appreciated joy in their life? Especially if you are feeling overwhelmed, overworked, and overtired. So how do you do that?

Twenty years ago, I called it needing some more coping skills. Today, I would call it **building resiliency**. Has language changed over the last couple of decades, or is it me who changed? Either way, finding ways to manage your reactions (so you achieve more calm) and manage your emotions (so you achieve more joy) are pretty attractive goals.

Frequent suggestions for increasing your resiliency include getting the ideal amount of sleep, eating nutritious meals, and spending time with mindfulness and meditation (in addition to many other viable strategies). Hmmm! So, how achievable does this seem? Back when I needed it the most, I had sleep problems due to stress about not getting everything done or not doing it well enough. I recall waking up in the night, unable to get back to sleep because I was panicked that I wasn't a good enough mother, wife, or employee. Nutritious meals? Time for meditation? Heck, I couldn't even do the sleep thing right.

When the house is engulfed in flames, it might not be the right time to show up with sandwiches, housewares, and new clothing. Sandwiches and housewares are very much needed, but the timing might be better after the flames have been doused.

I agree that resiliency practices are key to sustained peacefulness and happiness, but timing is everything. These days, a decade or so later, I am very interested in my sustained wellness and resiliency—and have dedicated Section 4 of this book to building resiliency. Back then, life was much more urgent.

Looking back, I can see that each of the visualizations, thought processes, and therapy sessions I went through over the years were not only getting me through the fire, but they were also creating building blocks that would later become a part of my self-care and resiliency practices. I had to go through a series of changes in my thinking patterns and belief systems first. At the time, those thinking patterns and belief systems seemed carved in stone and almost impossible to adjust—but it did happen. Most of the many adjustments were probably so small they weren't even noticeable, but in the end, it all added up to be significant.

> "Each of the visualizations, thought processes, and therapy sessions I went through were creating building blocks for my future self-care and resiliency practices."

So, the lesson here is to stop worrying about not spending adequate time working on your resiliency. That can only lead to more worry, which shrinks your resiliency (rather than building it). Instead, reassure yourself that each time you manage to take a deep, relaxing breath (even if it's while sitting on the toilet) or smile at a nice view (even if you glance at it for only a second as you speed by on your way to work), you're leaning in the right direction—toward greater resilience, rather than leaning away from it.

These days, I attempt to meditate every now and then. I don't seem to be very good at long, formal meditations (more on that later), but I believe I have found a way to make it work for me.

Back then, when the house was on fire, a co-worker said that his wife (who had travelled her own wellness journey) found meditation helpful, so he gave me a copy of the guided meditation tape that she used. I really wanted to do it, but I just couldn't justify the time to sit still with it—so I listened in the car. Even then, I could see the flaw in that approach. Meditation is not intended to co-exist with driving in traffic—but I could also see the humour in it.

Thankfully, I have always maintained a self-deprecating humour. It gives me joy when people laugh along with me. The humour has also helped me find my way to the peaceful calm and appreciated joy that we are all searching for.

SECTION 2
Thankfully, Change Happens

Leaning Toward the Hope for Something Better

Change is constantly happening. Even when someone does not appear to be making any adjustments, they are, in fact, experiencing change, if in no other way than by becoming *more stuck* (or more determined) in their current position or opinions.

Think of a rock precariously perched on the side of a hill. It looks like it should give way and roll down the hill, yet it doesn't give in to gravity, so there seems to be no change—the rock is still precariously perched on the side of the hill. However, if you were to take a closer look, there actually **are** changes taking place around that rock. Possibly, dirt is piling up, and brush is growing around it, causing it to be more stuck. Getting more stuck[1] is, in fact, a form of change!

So, what's it going to be? Intentional change in a positive direction or staying still and becoming an unmoving rock?

There's a good chance each of us is thinking of someone else in our life right now rather than ourselves. We all know people we think should change their opinions or way of life. We can see it more easily in others when a person's life gets more stuck. It's sometimes harder to notice it in ourselves—and that's okay. Change will happen if and when it's meant to happen. No one else can push us into it. It will come from within—when the time is right. (Which

---

1 *More stuck* would be another example of my sophisticated terminology. Maybe I should start using a thesaurus, but I seem to be stuck in my ways...

also means that we cannot push someone else into the change we think would be good for them. It works both ways!)

If we are choosing to adjust some aspects of ourselves, I like to think of it as leaning in a different direction. If we lean in a certain direction, then we are bound to move in that direction. Try it! Stand up and lean your body forward. As you continue to lean forward in that direction, you'll notice that your feet can't help but follow—it's physics! It's also true if you lean your body to the left or the right; your feet will eventually follow, and you will move in that direction.

> "As you continue to lean forward (towards something better), your feet can't help but follow —it's physics!"

The opposite is also true. If we fall back and lean away from where we were hoping to go, we will most likely move farther away from what we had hoped. As much as we may be disappointed when we find ourselves leaning away from our goal, be assured that it's going to be okay because as long as we still desire to move forward, we will get ourselves back into that positive, forward-thinking mindset and lean into it.

Many times, we aren't sure what we are leaning into—all we know is that we are leaning toward the hope for something better. We may not know all the big (and little) steps required to make a change in our life, but leaning forward toward that *hope* will move us toward the next step (or hurdle), and we will figure out what to do from there. That seems to be the way it works for most of us.

How long will it take? Who knows, but keep leaning into it, and it will happen. In fact, it is already happening.

This section is about the various stages we pass through when making a change. The change might be in our thoughts, or it might be a change to one of our habits (exaggerating) or actions (smoking). For me, it was all about my mindset and way of thinking. Once I could find another way of thinking, the actual problem (my emotional overreactions) started to sort itself out. It didn't happen overnight—but it happened. It can happen for you as well.

I'm Not Part of the Problem, Am I?

Self-preservation is huge. It's a human instinct, and it keeps us alive.

I believe we are all defensive—which is a good thing at times. It's important to stick up for yourself—it's a part of our self-preservation. But it's also important to be honest with yourself.

I remember exactly where I was the moment I let it truly sink into my awareness that maybe I was part of my problem, and that maybe it was okay—very scary, but okay—to let my defences down. I can't remember the details, but I know I was reflecting on a recent argument I'd had with my husband, where I'd become adamant that my anger was justified. I was being defensive to the point of throwing a few extra (uncalled for) verbal jabs his direction.

The reason for the argument wasn't big enough to warrant the kind of reaction I sent his way. Looking back, I could tell that the more emotionally riled up I got, the more I needed to prove that he was to blame—not me. It was a necessity. I had to justify my anger and my mouth spewing out all that stuff, or else I'd need to conclude that I wasn't handling it well. And my "good" girl self-image couldn't accept that.

Ugh! I recall realizing that my over-the-top anger and defensiveness seemed to be happening much more than I liked recently, and it was making me feel like I was in the blame and shame column of the ledger, rather than the perfect and proud side. Yes, I can agree that there should never be a win/lose in a relationship discussion, but (logical or not) I really felt the need to stay in the perfect and proud column.

As I reflected on all of the messy bits—both the argument and my apparent need to never be in the wrong—I wrote myself a private note and hid it under my desk blotter. It said,

> "It's okay to admit your flaws. In fact, it's downright powerful to admit that you have parts of yourself that you are not pleased with and realize that you will be happier if you work on them."

Saying this is not a big deal. Many of us will say, "Of course, that's correct." But to say it in reference to long-held beliefs about yourself—about how you have interacted with others, spending a lot of time and energy justifying how you were right to be mad and act out on it? That's personal. And it can be scary to suddenly let your defences down.

For me, I had to consider that even if I was justified, my emotional reactions weren't what I wanted them to be—and that they were happening without me being able to rein them in, which is never a good thing. It was like Pavlov's dog experiment; the bell would ring, and I would (emotionally) explode. I was a part of the problem.

A psychology expert would identify this realization using impressive words. I don't have those words, but I know that realization was painful for me. Many times, I have pictured myself sitting at my desk in that corner of the living room beside the window, writing those three or four lines to myself and then hiding them under the desk blotter hidden by my keyboard. I knew it was true; even though I wasn't ready to admit my emotional-explosion flaw to anyone else, admitting it to myself was hard enough and all that mattered. That was a big step!

Over the years, I've looked for that little piece of paper. I've moved my desk a few times since then, and I know there's a good chance I tucked it away in a file folder. I know I would've kept it because it was so meaningful to me, but I can't find it. And maybe that's just as well. The memory of what I wrote to myself that day might be more powerful than the actual note.

Dr. P's Stages of Change

Several years after I first started thinking about toboggan hills and the power of admitting that I might be part of the problem, I was in a planning meeting with two other peer support training experts.

The change model diagram (adapted from Prochaska and DiClemente's Transtheoretical Model of Behaviour Change) popped up on the overhead and I was awestruck. My experience existed within a well-known, evidence-based concept! It was truly a lightbulb moment that made a huge impact on me.

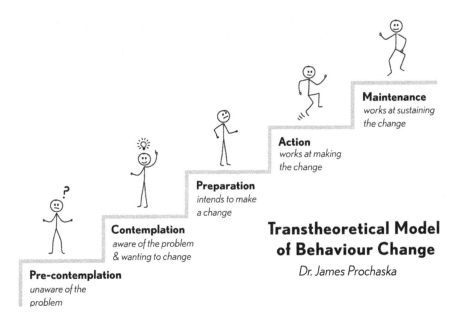

I knew with absolute certainty how those first two steps worked—at least, I knew how they had worked out for me.

Getting myself solidly onto the **contemplation** step had been a challenge. My defensiveness about my unwanted emotional explosions ("How could I be expected to react in any other way?") kept me in denial—and, in turn, it kept me in the first stage of **precontemplation** (being unaware that there was a problem). I could recognize it after the fact. For too long, I didn't even realize that there was something I might want to change about myself.

Turning off our defensive mechanisms and our "I was justified" way of thinking is not a simple on/off switch—especially in the beginning. It takes a tonne of courage to go from "Why do I need to change?" to "Could I change? Should I change? Will it be a positive step forward?"

There is a rationale for our behaviour in the precontemplation step. If we don't want to feel the shame or embarrassment associated with being in the wrong, then we must continue to be defensive. However, if we're willing to be super honest and wish to work on making life easier for ourselves, then we must admit that we've contributed to the problem. Whoa! That was a lot to take in for a perfectionist "good" girl who believed she must live life "the right way" if she deserved to exist. (Note that allowing myself to be mad was not a part of the right way to live handbook.)

It's like a fast-paced game of Ping-Pong, where you feel courageous and ready one second, and the next, you feel like the worst person on earth. To stay in courage and readiness to be honest, you need compassion—especially from yourself. You need to feel a sense of accomplishment for being willing to look below the surface and be kind to yourself as you work on forgiving yourself for whatever your most recent outburst might have been.

You feel self compassionate, courageous, and ready to take personal responsibility.
"I can do this. It's a good thing to be honest with myself."

Then, you berate yourself, believing that the last thing you deserve is compassion.
"How could I have done that? I deserve to be alone forever."

Back to compassion, courage, and forgiveness. "It's okay. I need to be proud that I'm willing to admit my flaws.
I'm a good person and I'll keep trying to do better."

"Who am I kidding? I'm one of those awful people who can't keep a lid on it. I'm a failure."

It gets so confusing. I think it's similar for many of us. I've heard others over the years, when in the middle of their own turmoil, speak with confusion as they try to explain what's going on in their thoughts. When I'm with another person who's Ping-Ponging all over the place, I try to keep track of all the competing thoughts so I can recap their fast-moving thoughts by laying them all out on an imaginary table for us to look at.

When my own thoughts are bouncing all over the place, I do a comparable exercise. I envision the thoughts Ping-Ponging back and forth within my headspace, and I try to grasp each one as it flies by so I can write it down. When it's written down, it seems to put it in a different space so I can begin to think objectively about it. When they're in constant movement up there in my head, it's hard to keep track, let alone stay with one thought long enough to give it serious consideration.

You must be wondering about my headspace by now—if there are toboggan hills and Ping-Pong games happening up there, where is there room for a brain?? Remember, I'm not a scientist!

It's a bonus if another person is also willing to be supportive and kind. For me, I kept it as a one-person, in-my-head, strange little conversation. It was bad enough having *me* wanting to tell *me* that I didn't deserve kindness or forgiveness. I couldn't take a chance on anyone else saying it—especially if I had just riled them up into their own frustration and anger.

However, there are kind, supportive people out there who are willing to listen with compassion and will strive to understand your perspective. There are also many who *get* it because they've also been in that same situation—that's what peer support is all about.

> "The curious paradox is that when I accept myself just as I am, then I can change."
>
> CARL ROGERS

Supporting Others

Something to consider: As you read through this, are you thinking of yourself? Or are you thinking about someone else to whom this might apply?

In my experience, it's the same for all of us. I know that no one else could have *told* me to change. They might even have tried (not that I recollect it), but I wouldn't have listened. I would have dug in my defensive heels and spat back with all kinds of justifications.

Therefore, I also know that I can't tell anyone else they should change, even if I have 101 reasons I think they'd be happier if they did. It just doesn't work that way—and if it does happen and someone seems to *change* because they were *told*, chances are that it might not be sustainable. Of course, there are probably examples out there that prove my theory wrong (which is good—I'm glad it can work like that), but there are tonnes of well-documented examples and research-based evidence proving it right. A person must first believe it for themselves before change can happen and be sustainable.

So, what do we do if we truly want to help someone? While it may seem counterproductive, we need to support them and love them just as they are. We strive to understand their perspective. Let me be clear: I'm not suggesting you should take their side in the "fight." Rather, you should strive to be open-minded, non-judgmental, and kind. That can be really hard to do, but being compassionate and supportive is key.

We are also authentic and honest with them—it'll be obvious if you state obligatory agreements and don't mean them. However, you can compassionately say something like, "Hmmm. I never thought about it that way. I think I see what you are trying to say. I'm not sure I would draw those conclusions if it were me, but I think I better understand why you do." And you maintain your own boundaries. You get to decide what it is you are okay with, and what you are not okay with. You compassionately maintain these boundaries because you, your day-to-day life, and your feelings are equally important.

> "When a person feels that they are truly accepted by another, as they are, then they are free to move . . . to begin to think about how they want to change, how they want to grow, how they can become different, how they might become more of what they are capable of being."
>
> THOMAS GORDON, 1970; 1975; 2000

I love this quote. I think it says it all. However, please note that change is not going to happen in a week or a month, or maybe not even in a year or two (*and possibly never*). Change takes time; at least, the noticeable changes seem to take a long time. But lots of minute little adjustments are likely happening along the way.

None of this—whether it's happening inside of me or within others while I am patiently watching and waiting—is just one big on/off switch. It's a whole series of thinking patterns, opinions, beliefs, mindsets, habits, and reactions that all fit together. Think of it as a really fine-tuned dimmer switch that can adjust the lighting so minutely that you cannot tell that the room is getting brighter—yet it is, in fact, getting brighter, just a bit at a time.

It's already happening. Can you feel it? Keep leaning in that direction . . .

The Next Moment, and Then the Next One After That

As much as we would like to believe that the change process is as simple as 1) deciding you wish to make a change and 2) voila, the change happens, that isn't realistic. Adjusting our actions and reactions—which actually makes change happen—is a trial-and-error process. It might feel like we make a speck of progress one day and then seem to lose it all the next day. The reality is that we're exploring and adjusting every step of the way. You'll eventually start to see adjustments to your thought processes, self-talk, and, finally, your actions.

So the question becomes: How do you cope as you go through the process? What do you do when you miss the other pathway down the hill and find yourself on that same old unwanted reaction path? I've been there, both as the person on the toboggan and as the bystander attempting to offer support.

Several times over the past, I've found myself on the phone with someone who is attempting to calm themselves down after they've had an explosive outburst of emotion. It might be hours of anger or hours of anxious crying. Either way, it is painful and difficult to come out of—I can relate to that.

Once the worst of the outburst (or implosion) of emotion is over, it can be challenging to figure out what to do next. At that point, there is a strong desire for the person to try to "fix" all that has gone wrong. However, that seldom happens successfully for me as our emotions are still on high alert, and our logic is very slow to come back to the forefront. (It takes a while for logic to climb out of the trunk of the car and get back in the front seat.) The best we can expect of ourselves is to rest and recover from the storm—and to try to offer ourselves kindness and compassion. There will be other moments in the future better suited for clear thinking and meaningful discussion.

My advice has been to just get through the next moment without the roil of emotion . . . oops, that moment's gone, let's try another moment . . . and now again, here's another moment.

Each moment is difficult, but it's a whole lot easier to consider the speck of time ahead of you rather than to look back at what has happened in the recent past. . . Here's another chance to try again—it's another moment. Way to go! Try again for another moment.

"Even though it might be difficult, just try to get through the next speck of time without the roil of emotion."

Corny, I know, but true! If we can break a terrible period of time into current moments and focus on just the next moment that is happening *now*, then we stand a chance of having a better moment. If you can do it again for another moment, you just might get on a roll of *okay* moments instead of horrible moments.

Another challenge that goes along with this is what to do with the other person who might have gotten caught up in your exploding emotion. My tendency used to be to try to explain myself so I didn't appear to be so awful and illogical. That was almost always a mistake, as I couldn't explain my perspective without the emotion inside me getting riled up again. For me, it was always better to just stop talking!

However, the problem is that if I just stopped and tried to feel okay again, I would worry that by trying to resume a "normal" way of being, I might be viewed as getting off too easy (after having riled everyone else up) and not punishing myself enough. I somehow thought I deserved to suffer a little after what I had done (which isn't necessarily helpful thinking when the goal is to feel better for the sake of all involved.) I eventually realized that even if it appeared that I was getting back to feeling normal too quickly and easily, it was still easier on all others around me to have me closer to peaceful normalcy than anything else.

That would be when that *next moment* thinking would be helpful. If I could just get through the next moment, being somewhat calmer in my emotions, that would be a good thing. And if I failed, don't worry because here comes another moment to try again!

"It always feels impossible until it's done."

NELSON MANDELA

Running Away from Home—Adult Style

One day in particular, the house was too full of stress and frustration—most of it mine. I could not find my calm and was having a hard time keeping it together. I needed a walk—a long, energetic walk to blow off some steam. I told my husband I was going for a walk, to which he readily agreed (probably happy to see me go), and I took off through the front door.

As I walked down the driveway and straight through to the street in front of us, I decided I needed to go for a longer walk than normal and get outside the neighbourhood—I wasn't sure where exactly, but it was going to be a long walk. I recall thinking that I'd walk straight forward (which happened to be north) through the various parks and roadways until I *wanted* to come back home.

Eventually, I noticed it felt freeing to know I could keep going for as long as I wanted. It even became kind of fun to decide that I was doing my version of running away from home by going forward in the same direction until I felt *ready* to turn around and go back.

At first, of course, I went through all the frustrations until I eventually blew off the pent-up steam that needed to escape my thoughts. It was good the pent-up stress was escaping by walking alone, rather than by trying to manage it while back at home with family. I'm not sure where my thoughts went during that walk, but I recall trying to decide at certain points if this was where I was going to turn around or not. I kept going for a long while until I lost interest in getting away from the house and started wanting to be back at home with my family.

They say that taking a walk, especially in nature, is a form of self-care. When we do our various workshops, one of the exercises we do is to have each participant consider their **reactionary self-care** (what they do for themselves after a stressful situation) and their **maintenance self-care** (what they do to care for themselves on a regular basis). Walking often shows up on these lists. Stretching your muscles, getting fresh air, or escaping the stressors you left behind can all be good reasons why so many people find walking helpful. If you are someone who finds it helpful, then do yourself a favour and take the time to walk. If you don't find it helpful, then it's not a self-care item for you, but I'm sure you have several others that work for you.

"Taking a walk, especially in nature, can be a form of self-care."

That day wasn't the only time that I "ran away from home" as a reactive self-care practice, but every time after that, I didn't need to walk as far before I started to smile to myself that I had done it again. I found it funny that I was a middle-aged mother with a respectable career who still found herself running away from home. It's a good thing to poke fun at ourselves—with me, I find lots of opportunities to do so.

Finding a Supporter

Several factors help us to make changes in our lives. As you know by now, two big ones for me are self-kindness (rather than self-criticism) and the courage to be honest with ourselves. However, the biggest one, in my experience, is having faith in ourselves that we can and will make the adjustments we want for ourselves. In other words, having hope.

Having a supportive and wise friend who has faith in you and your journey is huge. That support from another person can help you keep the flame of hope alive inside of yourself and sustain your belief that you will find your way through the challenges—consistently helping you lean toward the calm and joyful life you believe you are intended to live.

This type of *hope* became front and centre for me as I became involved a few years later in the world of peer support. Peer support is all about hope. When one person is truly willing to *listen* to you—to all that you have to communicate, even the stuff that doesn't get spoken—and then offer support from the perspective of "I remember having those feelings or experiences, and I found a way to get through it. I'm pretty sure you also will find your way to get through it," it is peer support, and it is powerful.

When I was in the thick of my yuckiness, I had a sense that if I said something to Denise, an acquaintance of mine, about how overwhelmed I was feeling, she would *get* it. That was before I had

> "Peer support is all about hope; about someone having faith in you and your journey."

ever heard the term peer support, but I had still managed to find another person with whom I could talk about how I was feeling. We ended up co-supporting each other on our respective journeys. It was huge.

Denise was one of the first resources I found as I started my change journey. In that first afternoon tea, I said something like, "I've been feeling really stressed and overwhelmed lately. I've tried all the suggested herbal medications, but nothing seems to help. Do you have any suggestions?" From that opening comment came yoga classes where I learned how to totally relax, the name of a therapist whom I spent many years seeing, and many long talks comparing thoughts and helping each other along—and, of course, hope that it was all gonna be okay. There was more to it than that, but these were steps in the right direction.

In reality, what Denise gave me was *permission* and a sense that *I wasn't alone*. Permission is a strange word, and it wasn't as obvious as that. By her saying that she also had tough times and that seeing a therapist was helpful, I felt like what I was going through was not extraordinarily unique, and that it was acceptable to talk to a therapist. She normalized what I was experiencing and helped me to feel like it was okay to come out of hiding and actively search for a path forward.

It became a mainstay piece of advice for me to recommend that each of us find a supporter to walk the path with us. It may be a series of people, rather than one particular friend. It may be a certified peer supporter, or a random person that you first met at a parenting class. It may be your sibling or close relative, but it will more likely be someone who has not already been walking through life alongside you. Whoever it is, you will know they are the right person if you feel safe enough to be totally honest. Google "peer support near me" and see what comes up.

Reach for What Works for YOU– Books and Audiobooks

Listening to and reading books has been a big part of my journey, especially at the beginning. Some days, they kept me sane, and at other times, they helped me to be open to considering a new way of thinking. Apparently, I'm not the only one, as the personal transformational nonfiction genre of books is a consistent big seller.

For you, it may or may not be books that are at the forefront of what gets you through the day. What is important is that you keep your mind open to whatever it is that helps you to feel like you are getting nuggets of gold filling in those spaces where you have been longing for answers. If it helps you to lean forward with hope and anticipation for something better, then it's right for you.

> "If it feels like you are getting nuggets of gold filling in spaces where you have been longing for answers, then it is right for you."

I have lots of favourite books and audio recordings, but I'm only sharing the top four, the ones that had the biggest impact in the early days of my journey. A lesson exists in every book—even if the lesson is that you will never try what they are selling, it's still helping you to determine what feels right for you and your journey.

Recently, I heard an interview with Jeremy Lin (who is an NBA star I'd never heard of until he popped up in front of me on *The Daily Show* with Trevor Noah one night). His description of how he manages his struggle with fear and anxiety went something like this: "If I'm not talking to myself, then I'm listening to myself, and when I listen to myself, I listen to a lot of the doubts, the fears, a lot of the things that aren't true, that haven't happened, that won't happen . . . and the next thing I know, I'm going down this rabbit hole of catastrophic thoughts in my mind."

This felt very familiar to me. I'm not 6 feet tall and can't dunk baskets, but I know that if I allow myself to listen to the doubts and fears that sometimes play in my mind, then I'll also find that rabbit hole. That's why I often have audiobooks and podcasts talking to me when I'm alone with my thoughts.

If I can relate to and appreciate what I'm listening to then I find I feel more hopeful and energetic for what might be coming my way. I'm not exactly sure what appealed to me when I first started reading and listening, but I do know it was introducing a new way of thinking about life and the various challenges that popped up— and it felt promising and hopeful. That's a good enough reason.

These days, there are many current resources available through social media. These initial books and audiobooks that appealed to me are pillars in transformational self-help and, in many cases, influenced the more current authors and speakers of today. Maybe they will appeal to you.

Don't Sweat the Small Stuff . . . and It's All Small Stuff, by Richard Carlson:

This was my first. I don't remember how I found it, but it came to me at a time when I was too busy, too overwhelmed, and too much of everything to even take a few minutes to read a book. I kept it in the bathroom and read a page every time I visited. That's what worked for me.

This book was the first to help me become more self-aware and realize that I had a constant stream of self-talk happening in my head. That was a huge leap forward—to realize that my thoughts and belief system were as driven and judgmental as they were.

There's a Spiritual Solution to Every Problem, by Wayne W. Dyer

This set of audiotapes (*yes, audiotapes, it was that long ago*) was the next that I listened to. Dr. Dyer doesn't "read" his books; rather, these were a recording of a seminar he did on the topic of his book by the same name.

Many lessons were within, but the one that holds the biggest memory for me was hearing, "You cannot feel bad enough to make anyone else's life better." In other words, holding on to pain, frustration, and drama about something that someone else is going through cannot help them. There may be actions that *can* help them, but simply holding onto the negative feelings because of what they are experiencing is not, on its own, helpful. My recollection of his message went something like this: "If you can show me that my sadness is good for them and will fix the problem, then I'll do it." My takeaway from this advice? Do what you can to assist in the moment, and then focus on living your own life fully.

This seemed to be the complete opposite of what I had evolved into at that point in my life. I recall feeling guilty because I might be living a happy life when someone else was not. This way of thinking soothed some of the many guilty feelings I carried around with me and ended up playing a role in my thinking for years to come. I am still as empathetic and supportive as I can be whenever I feel it can be helpful. I know how helpful and validating it is for me when someone else is empathetic to how I feel. But that doesn't mean I need to hang on to those feelings when I'm off living my own life in order to consider myself to be a "good person."

Conversations With God, by Neale Donald Walsch

This book came highly recommended by a friend and the title captured my interest as I was in the stage of questioning everything that I had taken for granted in the past. Of course, there is the question of whether these conversations came directly from God, but for me, that wasn't as important as listening to a perspective to see if it *fit* with what made sense to me.

My biggest takeaway from this one was a suggestion along the lines that the Ten Commandments were never intended to be *rules*, but rather they were a list of things that humans wouldn't desire or want to do if we were to truly live in God's way. For example, a person would not *want* to kill, or desire another person's spouse, or steal if they had love in their heart. (*You may or may not find comfort in thinking about God. If preferable, use the word "love" instead of God.*)

That made a lot of sense to me. I get that. When I feel completely wonderful, grateful, and loving, I want everyone in this world to be happy and to have all that life can offer them. I have never felt bad enough to want to kill, or steal, or covet (thankfully), but I've had some pretty difficult times when loving-kindness was not the predominant thought. I also know how good it can feel to have warm and loving feelings for the people around me—I much prefer those loving and hopeful thoughts.

That sounds like something that I would love God to say—and we know that the Bible was written eons ago by humans who did their best to tell stories to inspire love, kindness, fairness, and faith, but for me, it's helpful to think that maybe they got a few things translated not quite the way they were intended. I personally react much better to inspiring leadership rather than strict rules, so I'm going to hang onto this one and the other tidbits I picked up from this book.

I Can Do It, by Louise Hay

I've worn this CD out. I went for years (possibly four or five years) playing it every morning while I dressed for the day. I would wait for my husband to leave—partly because I like his company and don't need someone else to listen to when he's around, but also because I was a bit embarrassed that I listened to Louise and her discussions about affirmations every morning. However, I found that having her reminders repeated into my thoughts every morning helped the day go better. And I seemed to hear something new, or at least something that I hadn't paid attention to before, every now and then.

Louise is all about positive affirmations. I've got my own approach to affirmations with tidbits like, "You get what you focus on," but she takes it to a much higher level. And there's nothing in her thinking that I find to be a downer or confusing. So, what the heck, I might as well listen to her every morning and be reminded that everything I think and say is an affirmation.

For example, if I'm thinking grumbly thoughts, then I'm more likely to grumble through my day, and if I'm thinking grateful and happy thoughts, I'm much more likely to smile throughout my day. Maybe it's a bunch of hogwash—but maybe it isn't?! Might as well give it a try. Who can find a flaw in trying to think happy instead of grumbly thoughts? Thank you, Louise.

There are many other inspiring authors and thought leaders. This list could go on and on. There are other books that have inspired me, and I know that there are many more books, videos, audios, apps, etc., that appeal to other people. Each of us has a different preference. Whatever works for you and inspires you to lean forward toward your best life is right for you.

What Might Help Through the Remainder of the Change Process

Preparation, **action**, and **maintenance**—those are stages three, four, and five in Prochaska and DiClemente's change model. I did not forget about them. They most definitely happen. But for me, I find them to be more like a gradual hill rather than actual steps on a staircase.

Maybe you are different. Maybe you find yourself sitting down and writing out a detailed plan of how you are going to accomplish something prior to putting it into action. For me, however, I go through a whole series of contemplations, trials, and rewrites. I believe that when we are considering our personal habits, thinking patterns, and behaviours, once we are aware that there is something we would like to do differently (which occurs in stage 2, contemplation), the rest of the climb is like scrambling up a gravel path where your footing scoots out from under you in some spots, yet you keep trying to get uphill, looking for any branch to grab onto.

Looking back, I can identify some key factors that made a difference for me. The biggest one was consciously deciding to *be kind and compassionate to myself*. To try to stop my self-talk from saying it was hopeless, or that I should be embarrassed and ashamed for being such a bad person. (Yes, I hear that language too. It's as if we hear ourselves being talked to as if we are bad children when that negative self-talk is happening. I will apologize to my kids right now for any and all of the bad-children lectures I may have given over the years.)

Another key factor for me is *visualization*. You can tell by now that my way to make sense of concepts and/or to encourage myself to find a way to accomplish a challenging goal is by visualizing a comparison. Leaning into a new path down the toboggan hill, or quieting the Ping-Pong balls in my head, or climbing back up onto the wagon (that one is coming up in the next chapter) were my ways of making sense out of what I wished to accomplish.

The last key factor for me would be *hope*. Hope that it was possible to feel differently and react differently. I'm sure I picked that up from a bunch of little conversations with others (including my psychotherapist), but one of the biggest sources of my hope was from listening to autobiographies and reading books. Wayne Dyer, Louise Hay, and the various other authors who spoke to me would give me hope that it was possible to find my way to something different.

Another source of hope and learning for me was what I affectionately called "Oprah University." At one point in my journey, I was working from a home office and discovered that Oprah was on every day at 1 p.m., so I would have lunch with Oprah and her guests. Several spoke to me and made me more aware that it's possible for all of us to accomplish something big, something different from what we started with.

I began to challenge myself to consider what I learned from that day's Oprah show that I wanted to remember in the future. (Hence the name Oprah U!) Most days, I picked up something to think about, but some days, it was a challenge. I was probably the only person who didn't like the big Christmas giveaway days. Something for you, and for you, and for you . . . but nothing specific for me to contemplate that day.

Where does your inspiration come from? It's worthwhile to give that some thought and to surround yourself with as many of those books, shows, or people as you can. A source of inspiration will never be 100% reliable, meaning that you won't necessarily get a worthwhile nugget every time, but if you're looking for it as often as possible, it'll help you adjust to or maintain a curious and hopeful attitude.

Adjusting Your Mindset

Has it dawned on you yet that a lot of what I'm speaking about could be described as our **mindset**? I define mindset as our attitude and way of interpreting life's various happenings. It's our approach to life—more specifically, our approach to all the little things that happen throughout our days.

Watching Oprah with the intention of learning something of value is a mindset. It's perfectly okay to watch it only for its entertainment value, but I was in the mindset at that point in time that I really wanted to learn and grow. I didn't agree with each guest's values or approach to life, but they at least gave me something to think about as I became more secure in knowing my own values. I was in a mindset where I wanted to learn from every book, every speaker, and every opportunity that I came across—whether or not I agreed with their opinions.

Louise Hay's book of *I Can Do It* affirmations is also an example of mindset. The mindset that "I can do it" is very different than the mindset of "It's never going to happen for me—I was born with these strong emotions, so there's no use trying to change."

> Again, I need to interrupt myself to say I have no right to judge other people or their mindsets, and neither do you. There's a chance that as I speak of the power of affirmations, you might be thinking of that somebody right now who, in your opinion, complains too much, and that's the reason they have it tough. Stop it!! That is neither compassionate nor kind.

> It's perfectly natural for all of us to judge others, but it's not helpful. It's not even a good idea to criticize yourself—especially not yourself! Positive change is much more likely if you're kind and compassionate to yourself. You deserve to have kindness come your way. Everyone does.

In my title above, I refer to adjusting your mindset—which makes it seem like it's possible to "pick" a mindset. If only it were that easy—to pick your mindset like you pick which bunch of bananas you want from the grocery shelf. Like change itself, our mindsets are constantly adjusting toward more or less optimism for a better tomorrow, more fun or more fear, more of this or more of that—the state of our mindset depends on so many things, a lot of them seemingly out of our immediate control. However, for me, it feels like something worth working on. It's also closely linked to your resiliency. When you're working on your mindset, you're also impacting your resiliency, and vice versa. The more positive our mindset is, the greater our level of resiliency.

> "If you enter a situation assuming it will be wonderful, then it is more likely to be wonderful."

This reminds me of a story that I believe I heard in a Wayne Dyer presentation. An older woman who had lost her sight was being shown to her room in a seniors' home. When told she was in the room, she exclaimed, "I love it. It's so comfortable and beautiful." This caused a little confusion among her helpers, who asked her how she knew this without having sight. She responded that she had learned that if she entered a situation assuming that it was wonderful, then it was more likely to be wonderful.

Mindset is everything!

Oops!

There is one other stage in the stages of change, and that is referred to as **relapse**. I most often refer to it as the oops stage.

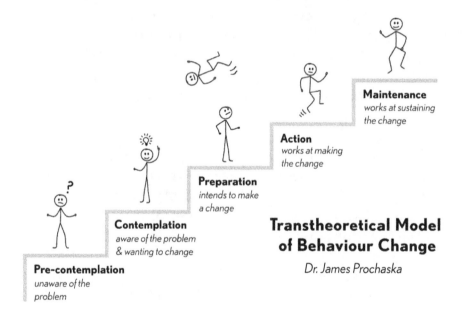

It wouldn't be realistic for Prochaska et al. to speak of change if they only considered forward motion! Of course, there are going to be movements back and forth and up and down those steps. That is what actually happens. How often does somebody make a significant change—let's say they are quitting smoking—without waffling between all the various stages? They've decided to quit cold turkey. Well, maybe a patch would be a good idea, or maybe they should just cut back and only smoke a couple in the evening. And then they pick one of those approaches, but it doesn't last more than a day, or a week, or a month, so they try another approach. And then that big party night arrives, after weeks of work-stress, family-stress, and every other type of stress, and their friends step outside to have a smoke . . . One can't hurt . . .

You get the picture. Slip-ups are much more likely to happen than not to happen. Does that mean that each one should be considered a failure? That would depend on your mindset! You might be tempted to say, "Forget it, I knew it was useless to try." Or you might try really hard (because it will likely be hard) to approach it as a lesson learned where you discovered another challenge for you to figure out how to overcome. Treat it as a learning opportunity!

I've never been a smoker, but I've discovered myself crying and/or shaking with frustration out in the middle of the field at the bottom of that (imaginary) toboggan hill, realizing that I had zoomed by the other path down the hill—even though I hadn't done that for such a long time. Or I've adamantly stuck with my version of the story where the other person was the reason for all that had gone wrong—even though I've gotten so much better at realizing that sometimes I have to take ownership for at least some of it. Or I'm back in my bed in the middle of the day, trying to convince myself that I'm not a bad person even though things did not end up as perfectly as I had hoped they would.

Every misstep helps you to better clarify what it is that you want for yourself—and how you might get there. They do have a purpose.

Life goes on. Change happens. And we're finding our way. The oops moments are a part of the process. Keep calm and carry on!!

Falling off the Wagon

As an only child trying to amuse myself in the next room where the adults thought I was out of earshot (yet I could hear everything being said), I would sometimes hear them speak of someone falling off the wagon—which would be accompanied by negative judgment in their voices. It didn't take long to realize that falling off the wagon, the way they spoke of it, meant that (in their judgy mind) someone who had a drinking problem (the term used back in those days) had slipped up and been drinking excessively.

Falling off the wagon had always been a visual I could imagine, probably because I often rode on the hay wagon out in the fields of Uncle Charlie's farm.

Decades later, during those times when "it" happened again—when, after the fact, I realized that I had suffered through days of self-recrimination or had made others around me suffer with outbursts of emotional anger—I would picture a hay wagon. I'd obviously fallen off my wagon and needed to climb back on.

Noticing that I was off the wagon would be accompanied by feeling like I had been rolling around in the gravel, head over foot, for hours. Needless to say, that hurts. I would feel pain in my head and my heart and my soul, and know that what I'd allowed to happen was regretful. But I had a choice. I could continue to focus on the shame and regret (or who I could blame it on). Or I could decide that I'd had enough of rolling in the gravel on the side of the road. It was time to climb back up on that wagon and carry on with the bumpy ride.

It's hard to pull yourself up over the edge of an old wooden hay wagon when you feel little and hurt. I could picture myself reaching up and getting my arms and elbows on the edge, then heaving myself up and pulling one leg, knee first, up alongside. It might be easier to say, "Forget it," and lay on the side of the road instead, but I didn't like it there—I liked it better up on top of the wagon. So, I'd continue to pull myself up and roll over the edge onto the flat bottom. The wagon would still be bumping along the country road—and I would just lie there for a bit. Eventually, I could pull myself up and lean against a bale of hay until I felt I had the energy and willingness to sit back up on the pile of hay bales and look about at the blue skies and trees gently blowing in the breeze—and feel hope again.

I know it's another odd one, but it was my visualization, and it helped me more than once to get back into life after a difficult time. I shared this story once with a young friend who was going through a tough time, and from that point forward, when we would communicate by text every so often, she would make reference to the ride on the wagon going quite well—or if it was extra bumpy at times. I could tell that her wagon was something fancier than my hay wagon visualization—she had grown up in the city—but it still seemed to help her, so I'm willing to share it with you as well.

Whether it's a wagon ride or something completely different, I hope my story spurs you forward to find your own thinking that helps you to recover when an oops moment occurs—because they will. Taking a tumble backwards means that you're trying. It's all part of the process of change and personal growth.

In the short, insightful poem called "Autobiography in Five Short Chapters," Portia Nelson provides an excellent summary of the process of change. If you're interested, it's from her book *There's a Hole in My Sidewalk: The Romance of Self-Discovery*.

The poem is easy to find online, and it's a quick and easy read. Print it out and paste it on your mirror. Change can happen. Don't lose faith in that.

Overcoming Reflexive Thoughts

As I write this chapter, I am in the midst of discovering something new about brain plasticity.

Much of this book, including later chapters, was written with my puppy dog laying at my feet or on my lap, but just last week, we needed to say goodbye to Baxter, our beloved dog of ten years. He had not been himself for many weeks. We kept thinking that if we just helped him overcome this next condition, then he would be back to his old self. Eventually, we received the news that Baxter was not going to be able to recover, so we tearfully said our goodbyes.

Of course, over the next few days, we had constant reminders of him as we moved through our house; we'd expect to see his face in the front window waiting for us to come home when we were out, we expected him to come running when we got cheese out of the fridge, and we thought about him lying at the back door, waiting to go outside to sniff around his backyard. That kind of *missing your dog* is fully expected and difficult to go through, but what I didn't expect was to have myself reflexively think about him as constantly as I do.

A full week has gone by, and I still have many quick thoughts relating to Baxter. When I step out the door, I wonder if he is behind me and also wanting to come out. When I fill my water glass, there's that 1-second click of consideration as I wonder if his water bowl needs to be filled.

This highlights two things about my brain plasticity. One is a reminder of how strongly those brain synapses are connected in our brain—"thoughts that go together, wire together." It is an actual physical connection of brain cells that's causing me to have these reflexive thoughts. I'm smart enough to know that my dog is no longer here, which is why it's only a 1- or 2-second consideration, and then I come to and realize it's not a logical thought.

Two is that I know, based on prior experience, this will pass. In time, I will no longer have instinctive thoughts related to caring for my beloved dog.

Noticing this has helped me to realize how this happens for EVERYTHING in our lives. No wonder change is so hard! Even when we want to change a habit or a way of thinking, those 2-second reflexive thoughts pop up all the time. We probably aren't even aware that it's happening. Not everything is as noticeable as a missing pet or person, and we have a lifetime to build up some of those connections that seem to be hard-wired into our brains. If you find that you instantly react with emotion to something a sibling or parent does, even though you wish you didn't, keep in mind that those neurons can be stubborn. Be kind and understanding to yourself. It may take a long time and a lot of effort, with several slip-ups, but change can happen. Neurons can be rewired.

While missing Baxter, I realized that reflexive thoughts had developed in the ten years since we got him as a pet. Thinking about filling Baxter's water bowl didn't used to be a thought every time I filled up my own glass. And, in time, those reflexive thoughts will adjust again and no longer cause emotional pangs for me. In this case, with Baxter, the emotion was grief-based, but I know that we all have reflexes related to the whole range of emotions: mad, sad, and frustration, to name a few. That's why I went back and included this chapter about needing to say goodbye to Baxter and what I learned from the experience.

The lesson here is to be kind to yourself and give yourself a break, knowing that it takes time to rewire your brain and break some of those old synaptic habits. At the same time, I encourage you to stay true to what you want for yourself. You can and will overcome those reflexive connections.

I will one day very soon fill up my water glass and walk out my back door without thinking about Baxter. It helps that he is not and cannot be here—no real-life relapses in this situation. But I also can look back over the last many years and see that by staying true to myself, changes in my mindset and thinking habits did happen. It may have been hard, day by day, as my reflexes worked against me, but it did happen. I did it, and you can, too.

SECTION 3
Learning My Way Through Life

Stepping Stones

Looking back, I can see the stepping stones that brought me to where I am today. In some cases, it felt like angels popping in to deliver some assistance.

When my youngest was a toddler, instead of taking him out for childcare, we found a woman to come into our home. Zaneta was one of those angels. She had her own teenaged family and was starting a new career teaching yoga. Providing childcare for us supported her transition. It was pretty obvious that she was a Type A personality (which I could relate to), but she also came with insights into healthy eating, yoga stretches, and the art of relaxation—which led me to attend my first yoga class with my friend Denise at the local city recreation centre.

OMG! I never knew how good it felt to intentionally totally relax my muscles—and I LOVED it. That nap that you take at the end of yoga classes (it has a name, but I can never remember it) changed my life. Seriously, I never remembered experiencing that degree of full relaxation and didn't even know you could intentionally decide to do it. If you don't know what I'm talking about, get yourself into a beginner yoga class—even if you show up late—just get yourself there for those last fifteen minutes. It's magical!

Around that same time, I was going to a chiropractor on a regular basis. They spoke often of the spine being the power system of our bodies (my interpretation of what I remember them saying). If our spine is in alignment, then the power is turned on; if the alignment is off, then the power is interrupted. Chiropractics didn't last—I found registered massage therapy (RMT) and osteopathy were more suited for me—but I did adopt the thought process of energy flowing from my brain to the base of my spine and beyond to the bottom of my feet and palms of my hands. My RMT, angel that she is, has reinforced that thinking and helps me Zen myself into a healthier body and mind.

I found my various stepping stones and learned from each of them. The above stepping stones (starting with something as unrelated as my child-care choice) set my path toward seeking ways to calm my mind, such as mindfulness and meditation, which has become an important aspect of my ongoing self-care.

My experiences could never be a recipe for you or anyone else to find your path, as we are all unique, but I found it interesting how the various activities and approaches that I tried each led me to something else. If you had told me back at the beginning that yoga wasn't going to be the full solution, I probably wouldn't have tried it. I went into it thinking, *This is it! This is going to change everything for me!* And to a certain extent, it did change everything, as I learned something from it and applied it to the next *solution* that I tried.

> "Stepping stones go along with leaning in the right direction. Leaning towards something that is sturdy enough to hold you temporarily and get you to the next stepping stone."

Stepping stones go along with leaning in the right direction. If you wish to cross a stream and you lean forward, you are either going to fall into the water or your foot will find something to step on that is hopefully sturdy enough to hold you temporarily and be well-suited to get you to the next stepping stone. And if you do fall into the water, it hopefully only results in a wet shoe and a slight irritation. Eventually, you'll get there—to dry ground—where you can continue forward, likely to find the next stream that you need to cross.

In this section, I share a wide variety of approaches and activities that made a difference for me and helped me learn more about myself and what worked for me. As you read, hopefully you will consider my ideas as possibilities, or better yet, something else will pop into your mind that feels like something you could benefit from. Lean into it and give it a try—you'll know soon enough if it's the stepping stone that you were looking for.

Parenting Classes—Doing It My Way!

I signed up for a parenting class back when my kids were seven, five, and one. One reason was because it was a night out with a girlfriend (yes, when we have young kids, this is considered an exciting night out) and the other was because I wasn't feeling like it was going well between me and my sweet little girl.

Like most experiences, this parenting class offered some valuable takeaways.

For example, I vividly remember Sandy, our instructor, talking about the value of giving a five-minute warning before it was time to leave a playground or playdate. If we, as parents, were suddenly yanked away from a super-fun social gathering and told to clean up and go home, we would likely feel some difficult emotions and possibly not react well. We would express our "No way. I want to stay" message in our own, emotionally driven way.

That made a lot of sense to me and, in hindsight, was a valuable lesson in empathy and the power of emotional feelings (and their reactions).

However, I also learned that I didn't always agree with the parental strategies being offered. I can't remember details, but there was discussion (and probably research) about how to set boundaries, rules, and other strategies for maintaining respectful momma authority.

In my particular situation, I couldn't see it applying. It felt to me like it would make things worse, in particular for me and my little girl, by introducing even more stressors. It was truly helpful to hear and discuss the strategies and the reasoning behind them because it helped me more fully consider why our situation as mother and child was different and unique. It convinced me that I needed to go with my gut and handle some of our parent/child situations in my own way—in a manner that made sense to me. (By the way, my way was softer and more lenient, in case you were wondering.)

In hindsight, I was establishing my own self-determination by making a choice that was best for me and my situation, even though it went against best practice. Those of us in the peer support world know the value of that kind of self-determination.

> "Self-determination is about making a choice that feels best for you and your situation, even though it may not align perfectly with best practice."

That was only one step in my motherhood journey, but it was an important and influential step. It gave me the confidence to continue to be the kind of mom I thought was best suited for me and my beautiful little girl (who's now a kind, respectful, and confident woman).

I have become a big proponent of the concept that parenting is all about individual relationships, and each relationship between a parent and each of their children is a little bit unique—and should be unique. We know that humans are unique beings, so every child is obviously unique, and each individual parent is, too.

It took a looooong time, but I eventually came to know that I can have a way of being with each of my kids, and I need to respect that my husband will also have his own way of interacting with each of our three kids. Of course, there's a degree of consistency between the two of us, and there is as much equality as possible between the kids (even though each of them would complain about it not being fair). This is a HUGE subject that deserves its own book.

I include my story about parenting classes near the beginning of this "Learning My Way Forward" section (which is all about *trying to feel better*) because it represents the value of determining what is right for you and your unique situation (which is what self-determination is all about). I found several helpful strategies from that six-week parenting course, and equally important, I was led forward into thinking more about the strategies that I knew in my gut weren't right for me and my unique relationship. This applies not only to parenting but to most aspects of our lives and choices in how we grow forward.

Life is a learning process. Keep your mind open to new ideas, have faith in your instincts, and keep leaning forward, ready for the next stepping stone.

Giving the Goofy Stuff a Try

There were a lot of years when I had horrendous headaches that would last for two or three days. But of course, in those days, that wouldn't stop me from attempting to do my job (at that time, I was doing computer training classes), be there for my three youngish children, volunteer (church, school, kids' activities), and be a good friend and family member (striving to not miss family events even though they might be two hours away on an already heavily scheduled weekend). Like every other perfectionist do-gooder (I know I'm not the only one!!), I attempted to keep the idealistic goals I had set for myself.

These headaches would come on quietly but persistently stick around with the pain throttle at full blast until they would finally disappear in the early evening, often two or three days later. I would load up on Aspirin, Anacin, or anything else that seemed magical, and try to keep going. I went to the doctor—she suggested maybe it was my pillow, which made no sense to me. I kept track of what I was eating, but I suspected something different every time I tracked it. My menstrual cycle? Nope, no link there. Seasonal allergies? That didn't seem to be it. Too much stress? Didn't seem like the answer, as I even got them now and then while on vacation. There had to be a reason . . .

These headaches continued for several years, even after I started to pay attention to my mental wellness and began seeing a psychotherapist. We talked about all the regular stuff for the first few months (mother, father, husband, children, work, back to my mother, and my father . . .) My therapist was a very quiet man (who

I truly appreciated—he was perfect for me) who was careful to do much more listening than talking.

I remember complaining several times about my headaches, and he would hesitantly suggest that maybe digging deeper into my psyche and life experiences might be the answer. I could never bring myself to agree to something that felt way too *woo-woo* and *airy-fairy*. I liked to deal in facts and realities. After all, when I started to see him, I was only hoping for more *coping* skills.

Finally, I relented and said, "Okay, I've decided to give your goofy idea a try." Yes, I did use the word "goofy." He happened to have been leaning back in his office chair at the time, and I remember him letting his foot give way so that he and the chair swung forward as he probably tried (but didn't fully succeed) to not react to my calling his profession goofy.

I'm not sure why I spoke of it as being goofy. I think it was a defensive tactic to make sure I wasn't becoming, or viewed as becoming, one of *those* people who need therapy. In hindsight, that was obviously a deep-seated belief that I held. I seemed to believe that needing therapy equated to either being overly spoiled with too much time on your hands, or being too mentally unwell to cope through life. (Just a little bit of judgment there—please forgive me; I've grown since then.)

> "Being willing to dig deeper into your thoughts and life experiences can be another stepping stone in the big picture of making changes and moving forward."

As it turned out, I did need therapy, not necessarily for the aforementioned reasons, but rather because having that opportunity to learn and grow was truly important to me. Once I started to notice changes and improvements in how I was feeling, I realized that if I hadn't emotionally fallen apart at that point in my life, then I would have continued to cope through life rather than truly live life with authentic gratitude and happiness.

Therapy—being willing to dig deeper, rather than staying superficial, with my thoughts and life experiences—was another stepping stone in the big picture of making changes and moving forward. Did it suddenly mean that I was headache free? No, not immediately, but it did help and was a factor in paying attention to who I really was and who I wanted to be. When you are not sure of who you are or how to get where you want to go, it can be a pain—literally, a huge headache pain that won't go away for days.

Listening to Your Body

As I lived through those headaches, I often thought I needed to find a way to allow pent-up steam (or pain or energy or whatever was up there in my head) to flow out through a release valve in the top of my head.

I finally gave up on finding the one thing that was causing my headaches and just decided that I was someone who was going to get them now and then. This meant I was no longer chasing answers, which also can be stress inducing.

I noticed that when I had a headache, I'd unintentionally scrunch up my forehead, squint my eyes, or tense my shoulders—even when I was trying to fall asleep. It seemed like I was trying to keep the pain from expanding, but that obviously didn't work. It felt like I needed to do the opposite—to relax into the pain and *be* with it while it was there, rather than fighting it.

So how do you do that? I gave the idea of a release valve at the very top of my head a try. It seemed like I had given everything else a try, so why not? If I needed a release valve in the top of my head, then I would give myself a (simulated) release valve.

I would lie down on my bed and visualize pain (hot, searing energy) seeping out through that imaginary valve. I would think about that opening at the top of my head while

I tried to relax into the pain and let it trickle out like a small river. I let the pain flow up and out, rather than fighting it and pushing it down. Sometimes, the pain would seem to intensify for a bit as I was more aware of it, but I knew that fighting it or ignoring it wasn't working, so it was time to try to be at peace with it and let it slowly flow out and escape into the air around me.

Keeping my thoughts calmly on the top of my head helped me to relax the muscles in my head, neck, and shoulders and to *be okay* with the pain. The headache wouldn't instantly go away when doing this, but it would allow me to relax into it, which, in hindsight, was what my body was calling for—some calm and relaxation. I was okay with it not going away instantly when doing this since being with the pain meant I was accepting that it was going to stick around for a while. Besides, I'd already determined that I wasn't finding better options that made it go away, so I might as well strive to accept it.

Giving in to the pain and taking time to rest (sometimes even in the middle of the day!) didn't feel right to me at first. My mantra had been that I could work through anything—snow, rain, or headache pain. I'd been telling myself the make-believe story that people were going to notice and admire my strength and perseverance, and I was going to be the best at it—whatever *it* might be that day. But it wasn't working. I don't recall getting any extra appreciation or admiring fan mail for doing it all, even though I felt like crap, and I was starting to feel more and more like crap. That approach wasn't doing me any favours.

Listening to my body and giving myself *permission* to take it easy was helpful—not an instant success, but it felt like it was what my body was asking for. The stressed-out voice in my head, who was in the habit of striving through it all no matter what, would try to call me weak and lazy, but it was time to try a different approach. Maybe I didn't need to be *amazingly strong-willed*; instead, I could just be *average*, and average meant taking a rest if it was needed.

This change in behaviour and mindset (going from a no-holds-barred approach to doing it all no matter the toll it was taking on me to lying down for a bit when my headaches were at a 9 out of 10 on the pain scale) was another of the many examples of a change process that was of benefit to me. Coincidentally, it also benefited all those around me who I was trying to serve.

Where do you need a release valve to let out pent-up steam, pain, or anger? Give yourself the gift of taking a few minutes to be quiet and focus on the part of your body through which the energy needs to escape. Is it the bottom of your feet, the backs of your knees, that area just below your sternum and between your ribs, or the triangle of bones at the top of your butt and bottom of your backbone? Listen to your body and see if there's a spot that's asking for help. Even if you can't take the time to do it in your day, try it in the middle of the night when you're lying awake, unable to sleep—yes, I also had those nights of no sleep. If this appeals to you, give it a try.

Years later, as I experimented with mindfulness and meditation (another woo-woo idea for a practical girl like me), I realized that what I was doing with those headache release valves was a form of mindfulness visualization, and knowing that I had done it before helped me to realize I could do it again, even without the pain. Those stepping stones keep lining up.

What's It Like to Do Psychotherapy?

Taking the time for a restful break when having a severe headache goes along with taking an hour or so every week for therapy. Both take up valuable time where you focus on yourself. Whoa! That could be considered by some (like my former self) as selfish and wasteful.

As mentioned, when I first started visiting a therapist, the plan was to drop in for a few sessions and get some new coping skills to take away. If I could just add on a few new ways to get through the tough times, then I would be good to go for another couple of decades—I was pretty sure about that. If I'd known at that time it was going to stretch into a much longer time frame than I'd expected, I likely would've never given it a chance as I'd have thought it wasn't worth spending all that time and money on me. However, I'm SOOOOO glad that I did do it. It became one of the most valuable learning experiences of my life.

Trying to justify spending time and money on myself was a constant challenge, but it didn't take long for me to realize that this was like a second degree. Going back to school for an MBA or another degree wasn't necessarily a serious plan of mine, but was something I'd considered every now and then. Spending time in therapy, for me, ended up feeling more valuable than another degree, as it gave me greater confidence and a greater capability to live my existing life, take on new challenges, and have more fun doing them. Isn't that what a degree is supposed to be all about?

So, what's it like to do psychotherapy? Are you a massage person? Have you ever gone for a deep tissue massage where they find a tight spot and dig into it? It hurts so much when they push on it, yet it feels so good at the same time because you know it's releasing some deep pain that's been building up for a long time. That's what psychotherapy was like for me.

Not all therapists are the same. I can tell from talking to others (who also love their therapists) that it's not like that for everyone.

For me, it felt like a deep tissue massage, where focussing on something would expose the emotional pain associated with it. Then, after spending compassionate time talking about it, the pain would be lessened.

Another visualization: It would feel like we needed to poke around (conversationally) until we got to the right spot, and then air bubbles would float up and dissipate. That deep emotional pain would escape, a bubble at a time, as I talked about (and cried over) whatever it was that needed to come out. Dr. Fowler mostly kept quiet—it's amazing what you will say when no one else is talking—until it was his turn to help me reframe whatever it was that I had found deep in my thoughts and beliefs.

I didn't go into it thinking that I had all kinds of emotional pain that I needed to fix or expose. But, voila, once I started answering simple questions about myself and my approach to life, there it would be—a long-held belief system based on my little-girl understanding of our world and how to live in it.

For those of you who know me, you're probably wondering what it was that got talked about. I couldn't tell you all the details at this point in time. I remember bits and pieces of the big items that kept coming back up over and over again. But all the little stuff that took up most of the time was just odds and ends of life—past and present.

It was like peeling back the layers of an onion. The outside superficial stuff came first, and then there was another layer, and then there was another layer. I didn't stop because I thought I was done—I'll never be done. I stopped because I felt I'd gone as far as I reasonably could at that time. I learned more about how to be kind to myself and how to reframe things into more compassionate views, and I'm now able to continue to learn and grow and help myself through tough times, on my own.

After all, change takes time. I am forever grateful for the patience and time Dr. Fowler had for me.

Finding the Right Therapist for You

Whenever I talk about finding a doctor or therapist, my advice is always to try three different people. I know we don't all have the luxury of having a choice of supports such as these, but if at all possible, go forward assuming you are going to try out a few therapists to see who is the best fit for you.

I went to a woman for three or four visits. It went well at first—I remember one valuable tidbit that I picked up from her. When talking about my daughter and how emotional and difficult some of our conversations were, she said that when a lot of emotion is involved, it sometimes doesn't come out in nice, neat, polite little packages of communication—sometimes, it explodes out. That was really valuable to consider. It truly helped me, in many a situation, to be as understanding as possible when someone else is unintentionally communicating using the emotional explosion method. It also helped me to better understand myself when I unintentionally emotionally exploded.

However, by my third or fourth visit, I sensed her restlessness, and she replied with, "As I have mentioned before . . ." Oops! We were NOT a good fit. With that comment, I felt extraordinarily shut down and hopeless. I obviously needed someone who had more patience with me for being (apparently) slow to simply follow instructions and fix who I was . . . Enough about her—I can feel my emotions building just thinking back to that. There is good and bad to everyone and everything—I took the good advice regarding explosions and got out of there once I realized she wasn't the best fit for me on an ongoing basis.

Even with my preferred therapist, who I truly valued, I had an opinion about what would and wouldn't work for me. He'd occasionally suggest that I might find it helpful to lie on the couch (which faced the other way) rather than sit opposite him in the chair. My instinct was to always say no, but I eventually agreed to try it . . . And I didn't like it—not even a little bit. As much as I trusted him, all that trust disappeared when I couldn't keep an eye on him and make sure he wasn't napping or rolling his eyes at what I was saying. No couch for me!! (Apparently, I still have some trust issues.)

Whenever I do a peer support training session, I include a hands-on exercise where everyone in the group has an opportunity to rearrange potential mental health support options that are written on cards and place them on a scale from most helpful to least helpful. It includes a wide variety of resources, such as doctor, work manager, emergency medical staff, medication, religion, etc. It's a very telling exercise wherein it becomes very clear how unique each one of us is when living our journey to better mental health.

A card with a support option like "parents" written on it might result in one person placing it at the very top of the scale at the most helpful end, and then the next person will move it back down to the least helpful end of the scale. It depends on each person's experience and preference. Therapy is sometimes one of those supports that's constantly on the move, from most helpful to least helpful to midway between the two, depending on who's expressing their opinion and who their therapist was.

For me, therapy would be most helpful—but just because the style and approach of my (second) therapist was so meaningful for me doesn't mean that it'll work for everyone. And if I had given up after trying that first therapist, it would be at the other end, with the least helpful options. We're all unique, with unique needs and preferences! If you think therapy might be right for you, then don't give up. Have faith that the right person will show up for you one day soon.

Exploring Your Deep-Down Beliefs

I always knew that I felt overwhelmed with all that was going on in my life, but until I started to dig deeper in therapy, I didn't realize that the pressures I was feeling were predominately from within. These pressures were related to my thoughts and beliefs, not my (external) responsibilities and to-do lists. While I was definitely a busy person, the feelings of being overwhelmed and unable to cope with it all weren't necessarily caused by external stressors.

As my self-awareness grew, I became more aware of little tidbits of beliefs that I had picked up along the way and incorporated into my value system and day-to-day guilt. They weren't necessarily on the superficial layers of my being, but were, rather, buried down deep along with all my other little-girl understandings of how to survive and thrive in this world.

We all have significant events in our lives that shape who we are. I remember being a sweet little girl of six years old who was saying goodbye to my daddy (as he knelt in front of me doing up the buttons on my sweater) because he had arranged for me to go down a couple of houses and across the street to play with my friend Johnnie. It was just me and Daddy at home as my mom was out for the evening at the spring opening at the local golf course. Daddy had stayed at home—in his scratchy-feeling, checkered housecoat—because he hadn't been feeling well for several weeks for some unknown reason.

My recollection is that he'd decided he needed to take a nap so he arranged for me to go to my friend's house and was watching me from the front door as I trotted down the sidewalk and across the street. I likely looked back at him and waved when I got there.

Later that evening, Mrs. Bratley brought me and Johnnie back to my house so I could get my pyjamas out of my room and stay overnight at their house. Daddy was snoring softly in the next room, but Mrs. Bratley wouldn't let me go see him (and if it were me today, I obviously would have done the same.)

I have no recollections of anything else until very early the next morning. The sun was barely up, and cool mist was still in the air when Mrs. Bratley carried me down the middle of the street. I think I might have been asleep when she picked me up to carry me. She was taking me home so Mommy could tell me that Daddy had died in the night.

That memory will stay with me forever.

So much changed in my life that day. My belief system was a part of it. Not only from the passing of my father, but more from the emotional chaos that surrounded me in the days, months, and years to come. I'll never be able to determine the specifics, but life obviously changed for me and my mom—and a whole new little-girl belief system was born.

My recollection is that I did fine. As they said back in those times, "Children always rebound quickly." Everyone around me was worried about my mom. I definitely experienced a lot of kindness and extra care and loving—but everyone was justifiably more worried about my mom. I was, too! I don't specifically recall my worry for her, but obviously the bottom had fallen out of my mom's world—in so many ways—and she was now fully responsible for me, our home, and our future.

Decades later, as I sat in my therapist's office, I felt very safe and unjudged talking about my father and feeling the grief (and guilt, anger, and fear) that had been pent up deep down inside for forty-ish years. I found it interesting, from a logical perspective, to discover that I was (finally) grieving the death of my daddy. I felt like I was honouring my little-girl self, who was obviously still carrying a lot of emotion around with her. She (my little-girl self) appreciated feeling like she had all kinds of loving attention and time to talk about what it had felt like, so many decades before, to simply not have my daddy anymore. That was very healing.

Taking the time with my therapist to realize that whatever feelings arose were warranted simply because I was feeling them kind of blew my mind—it was like a breath of fresh air. Sad and mad were not necessarily *bad* feelings; they were just uncomfortable feelings.

Another deep belief that I believe was fermented that day is my feeling responsible for the mood of others around me. Over the decades, it evolved to be an unconscious belief that it was my responsibility to keep those around me content and happy—to the point that they needed to be happy in order for me to be okay.

As I look back, I can see that I attempted to protect and look after my mommy's feelings (from the perspective of a little girl who really had no control over another person's emotions). Later in life, as an adult, with my own husband, children, relatives, and friends, I could no longer function under the weight of trying to ensure that all were "happy."

Many of us with busy lives feel overwhelmed on a regular basis, which can be challenging to our day-to-day emotions and energy levels. But I was one of those people who managed to take it to an extra level by subconsciously believing that everything would fall apart and/or my love and safety within my family would be at risk if I couldn't manage to have each individual around me be okay with how their life was going.

Like most misguided little-girl belief systems, that's a bunch of hogwash—and it was fairly easy to realize that from a logical perspective once it became exposed and I could talk about it. There isn't a way one person can manage the emotions of others around them. Likewise, if the others around you are having emotionally hard times that does not necessarily equate to you no longer being deserving of love and harmony.

But the thing with subconscious belief systems is that they impact your thoughts and emotions without you even realizing it's happening. I felt like a slow learner, as I seemed to continuously talk about something that was bothering me, and my therapist would patiently point out that it was related to that same deep-down belief. *Remind me again—I don't need to feel like I'm failing if another person isn't feeling happy.*

It seemed to take a long time before I could identify, on my own, when current frustrations were somehow linked to this belief. Then, there was the herculean task of adjusting the belief and the impact it carried. Just because it's logical doesn't mean it's a quick fix. Like most change processes, dismantling the habitual thinking patterns (which, in fact, are neural pathways in our brain) that had been creeping into my daily life took time and persistence.

> "The thing with subconscious belief systems is that they impact your thoughts and emotions without you even realizing it's happening."

The reality is that we humans are made up of almost an infinite number of complex belief systems. Becoming more aware of the deep-down beliefs that may no longer be serving you can lift a lot of internal pressure off you. We all have them—you aren't alone in this.

It's also helpful to be kind to the little person within you, and honour some of the experiences that little person went through. For some, my story, in comparison to yours, may seem like a walk in the park. For others, you may be tempted to minimize your own life experiences because it doesn't feel like they warrant concern in comparison. But none of that matters when it comes to trying to feel better now, today. If something felt big to you, then it was big—even if the adults in your life back then (or possibly even still today) say otherwise.

If the opportunity comes for you to poke around inside yourself with a trusted other, it can be enlightening to see what long-ago (little-person) belief systems have become lodged into your day-to-day emotional reactions and thinking patterns. I highly recommend it.

Throwing out the Rule Book

I grew up with a self-imposed rule book. Of course, that's not really true, but in those overwhelming years, it started to feel that way.

One of those deep-down beliefs I discovered was my need to be a "good" person. It was tied in pretty tight with my right to live. Why did I deserve to be on this earth if I wasn't going to be a good person? (That's a big extrapolation—something else to work on.)

I come from a large extended family who are energetic, hardworking, and extraordinarily giving with their volunteer time, so I felt I had the recipe for how to be a good person. Throw in a few child-rearing books, and you've got an over-the-top list of expectations.

No one forced those expectations on me. In fact, my husband would say more than once, "You can't do it all, Kim," but my response would be pure frustration that he wasn't supporting me to do it all—rather than to give it some logical thought.

As much as I tried and drove myself to do better, it never felt like enough. Even if I had a day or two where I could be proud of all I'd accomplished, it wasn't sustainable. It might've been sustainable for another person, but for me, with all that was going on in my psyche, I couldn't do it all—and even if I could, it was never going to be enough.

When it came to be that I was overwhelmed and not handling it well—mad and sad had become my constant companions—I had to rethink my day-to-day life. I was just about ready to emerge from that precontemplation stage in the stages of change and was tiptoeing into contemplation. Like it always is (for me), there was a lot of Ping-Ponging: *Do I really need to make some changes in my life? Or do I just need to work harder at being successful as a good person?* Finally, I started to realize that it was my mindset—my *gotta do it all to be a good person* mindset—that was driving my to-do (and things to feel guilty about) lists.

I was starting to notice that *doing it all* for the world around me was at the expense of spending quality time with my husband, my kids, and mostly myself—and my mood and sleep were being affected. I wasn't sleeping well, often taking hours to fall asleep or not going back to sleep if waking in the night. All those expectations I'd put on myself were starting to feel like a book of rules, so my mantra became "I'm throwing out the rule book."

> "All those expectations I'd put on myself were starting to feel like a book of rules, so my mantra became 'I'm throwing out the rule book.'"

Of course, that didn't happen overnight. You can imagine me going up and down that stages of change staircase over and over again, with shame at my side. Of course, I could find others to blame when the self-incrimination became too great for me to bear on my own. This went on for a while—after all, we all want to be good people. The problem is the definition of good.

Part of the process was to consider what to do once the rule book was gone—what was next? If I was going to let myself get away with not doing it all, did that mean that I stop *all* that do-good stuff or pick and choose from the list? I tried the pick-and-choose method, but that didn't work as I couldn't find much to omit. So, I dabbled with intentionally doing as little as possible for a while.

I dropped out of as many extra activities as I could get out of and settled in to do a puzzle instead. It was healthy for me—for a while—to put no additional expectations on myself; no extended family gatherings, no church (and if I did go, it was by myself without dragging the kids along), no volunteering. I made sure the kids were fed, at school, and in their activities, and I continued working, but I did little else.

Hmmm . . . have you ever heard the expression that the pendulum swung too far the other way? Doing nothing wasn't for me! It took some time, but I eventually rediscovered that I like to be busy. I just needed to approach it differently. I needed that pendulum to swing back a bit and rest in the middle.

Around that same time, my son was on a baseball team where one of the coaches and his son had the last name Goodenough. It's a different name, so it obviously gets noticed. Sitting in the stands watching the games throughout that summer, that word popped up every now and then on the back of their jerseys and was a visual reminder that I didn't need to be perfect. I eventually came to appreciate that striving for perfection was unachievable and, in fact, was more likely to result in shortcomings in other areas of my life.

My new goal was to be good enough. After all, good enough is good enough! I had to repeat that to myself many times over, but it eventually started to take hold, and I started to become proud of my good-enough approach rather than thinking that perfect was the only thing deserving of pride.

What is it that you're discovering in your life and belief systems that you'd like to adjust? Roll it around in your mind and experiment with different ways of thinking about it. Keep your mind open to unexpected cues in your surroundings that will give you something to hang onto as you lean forward toward something new. What you find may not be perfect, but it'll be good enough to give you the extra support you're looking for.

What Do I *Really* Want?

Another symptom that reared its ugly head during my overwhelmed, super-stressed, mad and sad phase was that I couldn't get myself out of bed in the mornings in time to get my young son to school on time. He was perfectly okay with that—but I wasn't. I knew it was "bad" behaviour for me as a mother—the opposite of the "good" person ideal—but I couldn't find a way to change it.

I still can't fully explain why I couldn't find a way to get myself out of bed. I know it can be an indicator of laziness, but I also know it can be a symptom of depression. Whatever the reason might have been, I would eventually get up, but it always seemed to be at the last possible minute, not leaving enough time to get his slow-poke self out the door on time to catch the bus.

(By the way, this is very embarrassing to admit. I didn't even talk to my therapist about getting my child to school late almost every morning for several months as it was too embarrassing. The school secretary would *tsk tsk* at me some mornings—and from her perspective, I couldn't blame her. I'd vow to myself that I'd do better the next morning, but I couldn't sustain it. Thankfully, my son has turned out to be an amazing young man who gets himself to work (barely) on time every morning.)

Somewhere along the way, while in bed berating myself for still being there, I started to think from the perspective of "What do *I* really want?" Up until that point, I was always following the rulebook so I could get closer to proudly living life perfectly. But that was no longer working for me. So, I somehow came up with the idea to experiment and see if I could dig down deep enough to figure out what it was that *I* wanted—and if I did what I wanted, would it be flawed, or would it be okay?

I remember sitting in my chair, seriously considering this, and thinking that I'd probably be an okay person (good enough) if I did things because **I really** wanted to and not because society called for it. And I remember lying in bed a few mornings, and instead of berating myself because I should be getting out of bed and not lying there, I took the time to logically think through what *I* truly wanted for myself. I had to work hard at this as it can be difficult to not simply give the answer that society (or the rulebook) would dictate. I worked my way through the various levels of what *I* wanted (again, like peeling back the various skins of an onion to see what lay beneath each layer). I found that I truly wanted what was best for my son. And that meant I wanted to get out of bed and get my son started on his day.

Trust me, this was not a thought process where the second thought I considered was the one that got me out of bed. There were lots of levels, and I patiently (without judgment) gave myself permission to experiment and see if my thoughts would lead me to wanting to stay in bed or if they'd lead me to something else that I wanted more deeply. That was scary stuff, as I really wasn't sure if I'd end up ever getting out of bed if I let *I* run my life. But I also suspected and had enough faith in myself to believe that somewhere down deep, I'd find myself to be a good person (or a good-enough person), not just a well-behaved person.

> "Doing something because you truly want to is so much more powerful than doing it because you have to."

Doing something because you truly want to is so much more powerful than doing it because you have to. It relates to the idea expressed earlier that none of us can expect to change another person; they need to want to do it for themselves. It's true whether another person is forcing their expectations on you or if it starts to feel that our culture is forcing expectations on you. What's really important is if you want that same thing for yourself.

Reading this chapter isn't enough reflection time to truly give this a try. But if the feeling that you're living life according to some big rule book of things you must do is something that strikes a chord with you, then there'll be a moment one day soon when the time will be right for you to sit still and quietly ponder: If you were to do what you truly wanted to do, would you still be an okay person? I have faith that you'll find yourself to be a very okay person.

> "When a strong thought comes and you are trying to figure out where it came from, ask yourself, Did that come from source and what my inner being knows about all of the things that I want? Or am I trying to keep something bad from happening?"
>
> ABRAHAM HICKS, *"HOW TO USE YOUR INTUITION AND BE GUIDED BY ABUNDANCE,* YOUTUBE, 2017.

This Little Light of Mine

When my two little girls were preschool age, they sang in the Cherub Choir at church. Yes, it was as adorable as it sounds.

One of the songs they often sang was "This Little Light of Mine, I'm gonna let it shine." The second verse was, "Hide it under a bushel, no! I'm gonna let it shine." And the rousing chorus was, "Let it shine, let it shine, let it shine."

That is great advice. Like all of us, I have a little light that is the real *me* hidden deep down inside of myself. I visualize it as a little candle nestled into the core of my body, just below my ribs (coincidentally, at the solar plexus chakra). Reminding myself of that little light inside of myself is really important, as I instinctively know it to be true. It's not necessary for any of us to *pretend* to be better people when our real self is good enough—in fact, it's perfect for us to be the happiest version possible of who we were meant to be!

It's rare these days that this little song comes to mind, but on those days when it feels like my light is more of a weak, barely flickering flame, I find that if I focus on slow, deep breathing while taking a quiet walk, and let an imaginary string connect to my lower ribs and pull them forward into my forward steps, I can feel more space for the candle to truly glow strong and bright. (It's interesting how I find the mind and body are connected—in both directions?!)

My massage therapist will sometimes tell me that the pain I'm feeling in my body is because I'm collapsed in on myself at my ribs. She prescribes deep breathing to expand my ribs and push those muscles out—I accomplish it by letting that little light of mine glow bright as I stride forward in life. *"Hide it under a bushel? No way! Let it shine, let it shine, let it shine."*

For such a long time, I wasn't sure that I was ever going to grow into the calm, confident, capable person that I so wanted to be. It was as if my flame had been dim and sometimes hidden under a bushel.

When you feel like you'd better follow a rule book dictated by culture and others rather than instinctively trusting yourself to know what's best for you, you've got a bushel hiding your light.

Reminding yourself that you're an amazing person just as you are, and you're leaning forward and growing into an even more amazing person every day, is a sure-fire way to toss that bushel aside and let yourself glow, strong and bright.

Another way I'd try to get my day started on the right path was to pick three words that I wanted for myself that day. A common choice was calm, confident, and capable. (It's only a coincidence that they were all C words.) Other days, I'd pick "clear" (if I had an important meeting to speak at). Or there'd be days I would wish for coordinated, constructive, and/or creative. (You can do a lot with C words—it became a bit of a game to pick a word that began with C, even though I didn't plan it that way when I started.)

Remembering and repeating those three words now and then throughout the day would help to set my focus in a positive direction and keep my flame burning bright. I have a friend who writes her three words on the mirror of her vanity every morning. I love that!

Do my words align with you and what you wish for yourself? If not, tomorrow morning, when you're getting ready to start your day, you may wish to consider what it is that you want for yourself that day. You're capable of all you ask for. Focussing on a couple of specific requests for yourself, like confidence and creativity, for example, can help to push the competing noise out of the way and allow you to focus on what you most wish to call forward for that day.

The warm glow of the light that each of us has within ourselves reminds me of my favourite chakra book, Ambika Wauters's *The Book of Chakras*. Have you ever had the opportunity to learn more about chakras? In particular, the solar plexus chakra? This chakra is the energy centre within our body that is linked to our sense of self-worth and self-esteem.

My favourite meditative reading from that book encourages us to unblock and strengthen this energy centre by visualizing a large golden globe that expands out from the core of ourselves as we contemplate our self-worth and become comfortable with the knowledge that we are worthy of the life that we want. Love, goodness, health, and prosperity are possible for each of us.

Let the warm glow of your candle glow and grow so that it warms you and all those who surround you. "Let it shine, let it shine, let it shine."

> A cute little story related to those Cherub Choir days. One Easter, after coming home from church, where the choir had just sung one of their songs (to much applause), we heard our younger daughter, who was three at the time, continuing to sing with great fanfare. Except that instead of singing, "Praise ye the Lord, Halleluiah," she was blissfully singing, "Cra-zy the Lord, Halleluiah." I thought it was hilarious that none of us noticed prior to her church performance that she didn't quite have the words correct. Oh well, crazy is a part of all our lives at some points in time.

Life Is Like a Golf Shot—
Envision It to Be Great

Long ago, before the overwhelming stress began, I was packing up my home office in preparation for moving into a new house. I came across a short list of the characteristics I wanted in my new home that I had made at the beginning of our decision to move. I'd tacked it up on my bulletin board and forgotten about it. I remember being amazed that all the details, such as "kitchen and family room together at the back of the house" with "morning sun coming in the kitchen windows," were a part of our new house—even though I'd forgotten about this list long before.

That was before Rhonda Byrne's book *The Secret* was released. This book was about the law of attraction—the philosophy that positive thoughts bring positive results and vice versa. I remember watching the movie by the same name and thinking of that list of new-house characteristics. It was also before I was introduced to the power of words, vision boards, and affirmations.

Long before I could allow myself to get into the woo-woo of affirmations, I remember reading an article and came up with "You get what you focus on." I wrote it out and put it on the bulletin board in my office and felt like I could truly align with that thinking—after all, it was obvious. My thoughts at that time led me to realize that the more attention I gave something and the more I worked on it, the more likely it was to come true. I was co-owner of our technology business back then, and it made sense. Think extra hard about something, work extra hard on it, and it's more likely to be realized. While my explanation today would be more about intentions and less dependent on hard work, I can look back and see my interpretation of the quote back then was another one of those stepping stones.

So, what do we mean by **affirmations** and the power of words? That probably depends on who you ask.

For Louise Hay, the queen of affirmations, it might mean looking in the mirror and saying statements like "All is working out for my highest good" and "I have the job of my dreams, a beautiful home, and love in my life." I personally am not big on mirror work and over-the-top super-positive statements (but if that works for you, keep doing it—or at least give it a try). However, I believe there's power in the words we choose. What we think and how we phrase what we say impact what ends up happening.

It's like a golf shot. When you first learn how to play golf, you learn about keeping your head down, your left arm straight, your thumbs pointing down in your grip, your knees slightly bent, your hips rotating when you swing, and making a full follow through, etc. That is a lot to remember! How long does it take to swing the club? Maybe a couple of seconds?? Is a golfer really thinking about all those details in those two seconds? Not likely.

Of course, practising the sport makes a huge difference, but once you have the basics down, you're more likely to picture the shot soaring through the air and bouncing on the green a couple of times before rolling toward the hole (rather than thinking about your elbow or thumbs). If you picture that impressive shot, your body kinetics are more likely to line up within that two-second swing and give you that shot.

If sports psychologists were to tell us to picture terrible shots in order to have the most success, we'd all try to do that—but they don't. While it's certainly not a guarantee, in sports (like in the rest of your life), you're more likely to get what you focus on. That's why you don't focus on a dud shot when you're swinging the golf club—or the tennis racket, or baseball bat, or any other tool that comes to mind.

In other words, life is like a golf shot. If I can wake up in the morning and be enthusiastic for (rather than dreading) the workshop or family event or new recipe that I'm making that day, it increases the chance it'll, in fact, be great. My logic is that if I visualize a great outcome, I'm also likely visualizing or subconsciously thinking through all the steps that are required to get that good outcome. I'm considering all the tough questions that might come my way in a workshop and pre-planning for a meaningful response.

I may still have some concerns and nervousness, but it becomes an affirmation when I decide to only think about the concerns from the perspective of how I can lessen the chances of them happening (and knowing that I'm capable of handling any concern that comes my way), rather than letting my fears take over. Going back to the image in Section 1 of who's driving your car, I want to have my logical, well-prepared self driving the car, with the fear emotion in the back seat—not the other way around.

During the workshop, if I were to focus on the possibility of people being bored or disagreeable, then I'm more likely to see examples of that and (possibly) say in my head, *I knew that was going to happen. I knew this was going to be boring.* Having those inner thoughts and fears does not help a person think on their feet and adapt to improve a situation.

> "Expecting and visualizing a positive outcome subconsciously focuses your attention on all the intricate details that will help you get that positive outcome."

Just like with a golf shot, good preparation and experience are necessary requirements, but also expecting and visualizing a positive outcome is more likely to focus your attention on all the intricate details in your skillset that make a big difference.

There's no guarantee, but this is the advice your sports psychologist would give you, and I believe it can be true for anything—a difficult conversation with a family member, a first day at a new job, or an unwanted visit to the dentist.

The way I look at it, I'm pretty sure this can't backfire—I'm pretty sure that visualizing a good outcome will *not* increase the chances of a bad outcome—so there's no harm in giving the positive visualization a try.

"Affirmations don't make something happen;
they make something welcome."

MICHAEL BECKWITH

You Get What You Expect

I heard about a cool research study where researchers gathered volunteer university students and put them into a waiting room where the décor, visuals, and discussion all featured a specific colour. Say it was the colour green.

Then, when the students went into another room to begin what they thought was the actual experiment, they were asked to view a piece of abstract art and specify which colour was most prominent in that piece of art. The large majority of respondents would specify the colour that had been subliminally featured in the waiting room. In this example, they would say, "Green."

When the next group went through the waiting room, the subliminal colour would be changed to a different colour, such as red or orange, and the results would switch so the majority of respondents would say that red or orange, or whatever colour had been featured, was most prominent when viewing the same piece of art.

I find this to be very cool. I cannot for the life of me find the actual study, but even if I made it up, I have a feeling it would be true. We see what we expect to see. If we look for examples of how our favourite politician is doing an amazing job, we can see examples of it. If we look for examples of how a mistrusted politician is misusing their power, we can see examples of that.

These examples can go on and on and on. If we look for examples of how the new boss is unfair, we will find these. If we look for examples of how our children are difficult, we will find those. If we expect our spouse to be unappreciative, we will be able to find an example of that. And, if we look for examples of how we have messed up in our own lives . . . voila, there you have it—lots of examples!

And how does that make you feel? Wouldn't it feel better if you had a good boss, good kids, and an appreciative partner? Take another look. If you try, can you find some examples of positives? Can you find some understanding of why someone might (seem to) be behaving in a certain manner? Maybe you can, and maybe you can't. But it might be worth a try. For *your* sake, so you can feel better.

"All will be okay"

As for you and your self-judgment? Of course you have messed up a few times—maybe a lot. But there are also some examples of where you've been kind, helpful, and impressive. Which way of thinking (good or bad) gives you the confidence and motivation to be kind and helpful today? Go for that kind of thinking—it'll be better for you and for others who cross your path.

In Brené Brown's "Boundaries" YouTube interview, she suggests something along the lines of if you assume people are doing the best they can (and not intentionally trying to piss you off), it'll help you to feel better. You might think that giving them the benefit of the doubt is very generous. However, it's more of a selfish act to think of others as doing the best they can since you're the one who benefits by actually feeling better.

"I have an abundance of loving-kindness in my life"

Several of my favourite self-help authors place great emphasis on how we feel—which emotions we are feeling—as a tool for enhancing our satisfaction with our lives. In other words, they strive to help us (their readers or listeners) to become more self-aware of what feelings (emotions) are impacting us in each moment. If the emotion isn't a pleasant or happy one, then we're encouraged to think or talk about something that'll make us feel better. That's what affirmations are all about.

I've decided that affirmations are like that colour experiment. If I say to myself, "All will be okay," or, "I have an abundance of loving-kindness in my life," then I end up feeling better—partly because I'm noticing small examples that make those statements true. If I can be tricked with subliminal colours, then I assume I can manipulate myself into noticing loving-kindness in my life— and that helps to make me feel like giving it back out to others.

As I journeyed toward affirmations, I found that I couldn't easily jump in with the super positive right away, but I'd find affirmative statements that I could believe and repeat to myself. For example, I'd say, "I'm figuring out how to do this," or, "My life is becoming a bit more rewarding every day." Those were statements I could believe—and they made me feel better in those moments.

"I'm figuring out how to do this"

I learned more about the power of words while watching Oprah one day. Someone in the audience said something along the lines of "My life is never going to get better." I forget what the discussion of the day was, and I even forget what it was exactly that the woman said, but I do remember Oprah taking a moment to stop and work with the woman to phrase it differently (such as "My life will get better and better every day") before carrying on with the show. In Oprah's words (as I remember them), words are powerful, and you want to be careful about which words you leave floating around out there in the universe.

Research that, in my mind, concludes the same thing is the Sapir-Whorf hypothesis. It proposes that the particular language one speaks influences the way one thinks about reality. In other words, citizens of two cultures may have different mindsets and/or perspectives about life's happenings in part due to the language that each speaks. Can this linguistic relativity theory be applied to people who strive to speak (and think) in a way that emphasizes positivity rather than negative perspectives?

"My life is becoming a bit more rewarding every day."

These days, I think of the practice of affirmations as a language. I've become very aware of the wisdom of phrasing things in a more positive and hopeful manner. Some of you may speak French or Spanish; I personally am working hard to become fluently hopeful and positive—both verbally and in my inner thoughts.

If we language what we say in an optimistic, hope-filled manner (rather than a negative, hopeless manner), we may not be impacting ourselves immediately, but if there's a chance that it can impact our future in a positive way, then I'll give that a try! Besides, it helps me feel more calm and confident in that moment, rather than mad and sad, so I'm willing to give it a try!

All is good in my world today and always!! Are you willing to give it a try? Go ahead, say it with me . . .

> A great audio and/or book to begin with is *Experience Your Good Now* by Louise L. Hay. (Search for "I can do it" to find the audio accompaniment.) She provides an abundance of examples of what we might say to ourselves that is negative or based on fear, and then offers more positive statements to replace it with.

Stop Arguing for Your Limitations

I believe I first heard the phrase "stop arguing for your limitations" in an Abraham Hicks YouTube. They make a good point.

If you are in conversation with someone who is attempting to reframe your negative point of view or give you a pep talk, listen to how you respond to them. You might hear yourself saying, "But it's so hard and I just can't do it," or "I've tried. It doesn't work." Or any other version of you fighting back with how you are not capable of doing something. In many cases, what you're saying is that you aren't able to make a change.

I'm very aware that sometimes the challenges are stacked so high that they seem to be (and possibly are at this time) insurmountable. But keep listening to what you say anyway. There may be times when you find yourself being defensive when it might, in fact, be a situation where there could be room to be open to a different perspective.

Abraham reminds us that when we argue for our limitations, we are, in fact, speaking affirmations *against* ourselves.

I don't blame you for fighting back when another person is not being empathetic and/or is minimizing what you're feeling. That isn't helpful, and it can make you feel even worse. They'll likely respond by saying they're "just trying to be helpful," but I agree, it isn't helpful.

However, after that miserable conversation, take a walk by yourself and consider what just happened. The other person was not helpful, yes, I agree, but besides that . . . Is there a possibility that you are betting against yourself by defending your limitations?

Now that you're on your own, switch that thinking and do some self-talk that says the opposite. "I'm able to figure this out. Even though this feels super hard right now, I know I can think this through and find ways to figure it out."

Even if you have tried 102 ways to get around this obstacle and still feel stuck, that doesn't mean that you've failed 102 times; it means that you have experimented with 102 approaches and learned from each. You have learned a lot about the situation at hand and have also learned a lot about yourself. So let's continue thinking, knowing that you WILL figure this out eventually, and try approaches 103 and 104. You're getting closer to success.

Let's try an experiment. Right now, while you're reading this, say to yourself, "Everything's going to be okay." Say it again and truly listen to those words, "Everything's going to be okay. I may not be sure how it's going to work out, but I trust that everything's going to be okay."

Did you notice anything happen? I tend to notice a softening in my shoulders as they relax just a bit. Hopefully, the same is true for you. Do you feel your muscles relax or your stomach unclench—even if it's just for a moment?

This is an example of why we do affirmations. If you notice that you feel more calm, loving, grateful, or joyful when you make positive statements (whether it be with your inner voice or out loud), then that is a good thing. As we strive toward wellness, we are, in fact, striving toward feeling these feel-good emotions more frequently.

So what if it's contrived and planned! Whatever works to help us to feel happier is, in fact, helping to build up the neural pathways related to these feel-good emotions—and tending to this neural garden in our brains is part of what is needed for us to build resiliency and sustain mental wellness.

A brain shows noticeable differences for a person who is depressed and/or anxious compared to a person who is calm and happy. So it stands to reason that we need the calm and happy parts of our brain to be in good shape in order to feel that way ourselves.

Yet, the only way to build up those calm and happy brain areas is to actually be calm and happy. It's another example of what comes first, the chicken or the egg?

If avoiding tendencies to defend my limitations and instead saying positive affirmations helps me intentionally call forward the feel-good emotions, then I'm going to do it and imagine those parts of my brain happily building up their neural muscles.

"Choosing peace doesn't just happen; it's a skill that takes regular practice to master [...] Though you may never reach Yoda-level equanimity, devoting even five minutes a day to telling yourself 'I am all right in this moment' builds increasingly effective air-conditioning into your body and mind."

MARTHA BECK, *CHILL OUT! HOW TO OVERCOME BURNOUT*

Pink-Chair Musings

For me, a lot of this has happened in my pink chair. I'd better explain that . . . In our bedroom, we have two rose-coloured, tulip-shaped chairs that we purchased a way back while living in a different house. Over the years, they've made their way from room to room, being downgraded to less prominent rooms each step of the way. They're now in our bedroom, along with a little side table to hold our morning coffee.

These days, now that life is much calmer (the kids have moved out, and I consider myself semi-retired), I love having my morning coffee with my hubby, our dog Baxter (while he was still alive), and my newspaper while sitting in my pink chair in front of the sunny window. Over the years, I've found that a lot of my significant thinking time has happened in that chair in the corner of my bedroom at other times of the day. It feels the perfect size to hold me tight as I hide away to contemplate life's difficult stuff—sometimes in the middle of the night.

I've often sat in that chair, scribbling on a pad of paper in an attempt to get to the bottom of what was really bothering me. Or I've seriously contemplated how to be a better person (that would be old language) and tried to figure out what was happening inside of me that caused me to lash out with words of anger—hence my toboggan hill.

I have also tallied my lists of Christmas gifts while in my pink chair to make sure that each of the three kids were treated fairly, and I have experimented with my first attempts at meditation, setting the timer for ten minutes to see if I could last that long.

Most recently, I've tried to wrangle the somewhat competing theories of affirmations and psychoanalytic thinking.

A long time ago, I decided that I was someone who benefited from spending time with a psychoanalytic therapist, even though my affirmation-heavy self-help books and speakers pooh-poohed the idea of spending time focussed on the sad things in life since (according to their logic) this would keep me in a sad frame of mind.

Affirmation thought leaders would suggest that instead of talking about the past with a therapist, it would be more beneficial to strive to switch my thoughts to something that would make me feel happier in the present moment, using a statement such as "everything in my life is getting better and better."

Psychoanalytical therapists might counter that you need to uncover the past in order to heal from it.

So, which approach will result in a better future?

Is it wise to focus on the past and attempt to better understand why you're feeling the way that you do, or to focus on your present feelings and affirm that all is okay and getting better, moment by moment?

In my opinion (and experience), I believe both approaches have a time and place where they can be extraordinarily valuable.

I believe there is a time when it is wise to honour yourself and your feelings. This means nurturing yourself as you try to figure out why you feel sad, mad, or scared. My psychoanalytical therapist did this with me for years and taught me how to carry forward doing it on my own.

"It is healing and wise to honour yourself and your feelings."

For me, this includes taking the time to honour my little-girl self, who is still very much a part of me. She might be feeling there's a risk that someone I love is turning their back on me. Or maybe she feels like I'm not doing enough (or good enough) to keep those who I love close to me. Or whatever else might be the deep dark fear that's haunting me (and my little-girl self) on that day. Is this type of thinking because my daddy died (and left me) at such a young age? Maybe yes, and maybe no. It doesn't really matter why; it only matters that me and my feelings are important enough to allow myself to feel them fully on those days when they overtake me.

For me, thinking through the tough stuff from a logical point of view will (eventually) lead me to an understanding of what deep-down belief is playing a role at that moment. This will then lead me toward thinking about how to reframe or update my thinking to something that is not tied to an unhelpful (little-girl) belief. I do this by creating an affirmation to repeat as a reminder of the updated or reframed thinking that I wish to take on.

For example, if I dig deep and discover I'm feeling sad or anxious because I don't feel like I'm succeeding at making another person's life happier, I can instead switch my thinking to creating a couple of affirming statements that'll help to remind me I'm a kind and loving person and/or I feel good when I am kind to others, and I hope that it helps them to feel loved, but I cannot take responsibility for their happiness.

Or, if my deep-down exploration leads me to notice that it's another of those "not good enough" fears that's at the core of my yucky feelings, then I proceed forward with ongoing reminders that perfection isn't the goal I wish to strive for and that being satisfied with good enough will bring much more calm to me and everyone around me.

In other words, using skills learned in my psychoanalytic therapy to dig deep and explore what might be the source of uncomfortable emotions leads me to develop affirmations that are directly related to resolving the deep-down source of discomfort.

I believe both approaches, psychoanalytic analysis and affirmations, were necessary for my journey. That may or may not be true for you, as we are all unique. But for me, if I didn't take the time to feel the deep, dark stuff from a psychoanalytic and cognitive perspective, then I never would've been able to figure out what the issues were that I had to work through with my new language and affirmations.

There are many tools in the "feeling better" tool box, and each one can be a stepping stone toward you feeling more calm and confidence. You might find that some fit together, similar to how I found psychoanalysis and affirmations to be two sides of the same coin. And/or you might find your own combination of strategies that work for you. The tool box is flexible; find what feels right for you.

If my comments above appeal to you, then find that cozy spot in your life, whether it be a pink chair or a bench in the park, and take the time to sit with yourself (or another trusted person) to explore your internal deep-down beliefs and adjust those beliefs that could benefit from some updating. Then, put the icing on the cake with healthy doses of affirming and encouraging thoughts and words.

Looking at Meds

I've left medication until near the end of this section on trying to feel better, even though it was one of the first tools I tried. For me, in my body, medication has made a big difference. I've been on them, off them, then back on, then weaned off, and finally, as of this point in my life, I've decided that I'll likely be having a (low dose) happy pill every morning forever.

A happy pill in the morning isn't the full answer—at least not in my experience. But, as I have suggested to others when they have been trying to decide if they should try medication or not, I found that my anti-anxiety/depression prescription gave me enough of a boost that I could then work on all the other aspects of my life that impacted my mindset and mood. When your mood and wellness are dragging so low that you don't have energy for anything—or in my case, I didn't have enough calm (non-anxious) moments—then it's VERY challenging to work on some new thought processes.

This can be one of the more controversial aspects of mental health self-care. Some people have difficulty finding the right medications that work for them, and others speak of the possible side effects and risks associated with medications.

It's vitally important to work with a trusted medical doctor with your overall best interests at heart as you determine what's best for you and/or if you ever think you might want to increase, decrease, or stop your medications.

I'm so glad I found the courage to talk to my doctor about trying medication—and yes, it did take a lot of courage. That was back in the day when it still felt shameful (to me) that I wasn't able to cope my way through life on my own.

After a couple of weeks, I noticed a difference in how I was feeling. However, I was knee-deep in all the other approaches I was also trying. After a while, I felt like I could go it alone and (after talking to my doctor) wean off my meds. After all, I'd never intended to be dependent on drugs—I just wanted to fix myself.

Studies have shown that both mental health therapy and medications make positive changes in the brain. It shows up in brain scans that the brain is impacted if a person takes medication, and it also shows up in the brain if a person works with a cognitive therapist. However (based on a study that I recall reading), when a person stops medication, the brain may eventually go back to its old ways. But when therapy finishes, the brain is more likely to keep the positive changes for longer.

My interpretation of this is that both are effective, on their own and in combination; however, making adjustments to beliefs and thinking habits (which can occur in a therapeutic relationship) can be longer-lasting. Medication will likely help (assuming it's the right medication for the right situation), but you need to keep taking it if you wish to continue to gain the specific advantages that it offers. (*Remember, I'm not a doctor or a researcher. Discuss this with your doctor to gain better insights into the specifics.*)

For me (and I am very aware that each of us is unique), I found the medication I was prescribed helped me. Yet I was also very aware that my beliefs and mindsets were also adjusting on an ongoing basis. Therefore, I went through a bit of roller-coaster, trial-and-error phase over several years as I tried to determine if I still needed to take medication. (*Again, let me remind you to talk with your doctor if you ever wish to stop taking a medication.*)

In the end, I found I was doing quite well with my emotional balance without meds, but there were a couple of niggling issues. One in particular was that too often, in the mornings, I would wake up feeling the unwanted need to consider what the purpose of life was and if it was really worth living. Thankfully, I could always talk myself into believing that "Yes, life is a wild and crazy journey that I want to be on," and once I got out of bed and started my day, I'd be so glad that I was alive and living life. But I didn't want to go through that in my mornings—I didn't think that was something I should expect to live with if I didn't need to.

So what I did was make a list of the three or four reasons I was going back on the medication and tucked it away in my drawer, with that particular challenge as one of the reasons. I knew there would likely be a day at some point in the future when I would question once again if I could do it alone. I wanted to have a reminder to myself as to why I had decided to go back on meds.

Over the last few years, I've met several impressive folks who (for their own reasons) decided to live life without continuing their medications, and they're doing great. Each of us is unique, and each of us will find our own best way forward.

You can see I make light of my happy pill. Why not? It's certainly not shouted from the rooftops, but it's fun to say, "Oops, almost forgot my happy pill," so I do!

Self-Care—Bring It On

Self-care is important, and we all need to do what helps us to feel healthy and happy. When we ask about self-care practices in our mental health workshops, participants talk about things like yoga, going to the gym, cooking, playing with their children or pets, taking a walk in nature, knitting, journaling, meditating, and a zillion other things.

Self-care is what *you* find to be helpful. It's not what you think you *should* be doing—it's what truly helps you to feel good or feel like you're healing. Thank goodness, in my opinion, the gym is not an absolute requirement to maintain our mental health—we might find that it helps with our physical health, but it isn't a given that we all achieve the same mental health boost from a workout. Another person would say, "Thank goodness we don't all have to listen to that drivel in self-help books." To each their own.

> "Self-care is whatever you find to be truly helpful and healing."

For me, many moons ago, I wasn't using the term self-care, but I knew what I needed to do to feel like I was on a good path. This would have included seeing my psychotherapist, taking my medication, and listening to my self-help recordings (to keep my thoughts out of the black hole gutter).

In addition, I had to constantly remind myself to not compare myself (negatively) when hearing about the activities or successes of other people. I knew that if I heard someone had volunteered somewhere, I'd be tempted to feel like I wasn't doing enough, and if someone else had a great weekend, I'd feel like I didn't have any friends, and if a third person talked about baking cookies and watching a movie with their children, I might feel like I wasn't a good mother—heck, I don't even bake, let alone do it with my kids. I never stopped to realize that if I was expecting myself to volunteer and go out with friends on a weekend, there would be no time to bake cookies and watch a movie. It wasn't even possible to do it all, but there was still a tendency to feel like I should be. Funny how logic doesn't apply when your emotions are running amok.

Things like therapy, meds, and emotion/logic check-ins hardly ever show up in our workshop self-care discussions. Most people keep it quite superficial—which is fine—but hopefully they are contemplating their self-care more deeply in the privacy of their own thoughts.

These days, self-care for me is different. I've changed, so my self-care has also changed. I still take my daily happy pill, and I still listen to self-help audiobooks (some things are consistent), but I also dabble with meditation (trying to do it on a regular basis), and I am very intentional about sitting and intentionally thinking through whatever challenge or uneasy feeling might arise (rather than sweep them under the rug). I find that taking the time to fully contemplate all the various thoughts that come to mind around a challenge is one of the wisest self-care habits that I have these days.

I also value the opportunities that I get to take walks. I enjoy a long walk with my husband or a friend, but when it's just me by myself, I try to be contemplative and even meditative when I am walking. Walking is a great time to stretch your leg muscles and let your mind relax. If you look for pleasant sights that make you feel content—such as the red cardinal singing his song or the water gurgling down the stream—it can truly be a deeper level of self-care, much more than just getting your Fitbit steps.

I'm pretty sure that when people say they love running, going to the gym, knitting, or any self-care activity, they love it because it allows their minds to go to a good place. I've read that any repetitive activity can be meditative. For me, that would include weeding. I know that if I (finally) bend down to pull one weed, I'll see another one right beside it and pull that one as well, and it keeps going (there's always more weeds to pull out) until my mind meditates away to another place. It may take me a while to get started with that first weed, but once I do, I seem to float away into another place. Weeding never shows up on a self-care list.

And then there's my dear friend from back home who does all her dishes by hand because she likes doing dishes?! Every now and then, when someone visits, they'll help to clean up and put some dirty dishes in her dishwasher. It may be weeks before she realizes they're in there. While she has never said so, it seems to me that doing dishes is a self-care activity that feeds her needs in some way.

We're all unique, with unique needs requiring unique self-care. Something more common, like taking a walk, probably results in a different feel-good outcome for each of us. In reality, this entire book could be considered self-care. All the ideas—big or little—that are discussed in these pages could easily fall into the category of self-care. The good news is that whatever our self-care activities are, they're helping us lean forward toward our right life.

The Mindset / Change Relationship

I've spent a lifetime feeling the need to squeeze must-do activities into the smallest possible chunks of time. Part of the reason was likely due to having a busy life for many years, but the other reason was due to another one of those little-girl beliefs where being extraordinarily busy was equivalent to being valued or important. A person who wasn't busy was not valuable. Ugh! Another deep-seated, ill-informed entry to be uprooted out of my belief system.

Back in those "all or nothing" days, I could sleep in, laying in bed an extra hour or so, but then go like a wild woman when I got up and realized I had too much to do in a too-short period of time. Of course, I was logical enough to know that getting up earlier could've solved that problem—I knew there was a better way, but I couldn't figure out how to sustain it. It was easier to make a joke out of it rather than figure out how to change it. I talked myself into believing that the extra time in bed or on the couch was self-care—as I truly was taking that time to try to find my calm and peacefulness before the inevitable whirlwind of activity and emotion as I tried to catch up for lost time.

> "Work on your mindset change, and the behaviour change will follow."

I had to work on that mindset (and resulting behaviour) for a long time. And, of course, it felt like little to no progress was being made for way too long. I was taking Portia's same old sidewalk over and over again for a very long time—did you get around to downloading the "Hole in my Sidewalk" poem by Portia Nelson?—but then it started to shift. As happens with all change processes, my wanting to adjust didn't instantly make a difference, but at least it gave me lots of real-time opportunities to think about and try lots of possible strategies.

My mindset shifted in a couple of ways. First, I was able to convince myself that busy-ness did not equate to value (and even if it did, I wanted to be satisfied with good enough). That's a very logical conclusion, but logic and belief are two different things. It takes time for the logic to infiltrate the belief and then lodge itself in your brain cells.

The other shift was in my avoidance habits. The base of that second shift was to find a middle ground between the all-or-nothing behaviour that I was accustomed to—moving from task to task like a speed demon with my heart racing versus sitting on the couch or staying in bed a little longer, telling myself I was giving myself a much-needed calmness break.

The end result is that I now get up at a reasonable time in the morning so my hubby and I can sit together, read the paper, and have our morning coffee. I'm fully aware that reading my paper is my new avoidance preference some days, but it feels more productive, and I've gotten much better at moving on to the tasks at hand on the days that it's called for. I am leaning in the right direction.

This is a great example of the interrelationship of mindset and behaviour and how changing one impacts the other. Work on the mindset change, and the behaviour change will eventually happen.

The behaviour is what gets noticed and judged—both by ourselves and by others who have opinions on what we *should* be doing instead. And yes, we can force ourselves to change the behaviour, but when the mindset gets noticed and tweaked as well, then (in my experience) there is a lot less self-disgust and chastising going on. Being aware of some of the many mindsets that are likely influencing the behaviour means there's an opportunity for more kindness and self-compassion to go along with encouraging ourselves to make adjustments to the behaviour.

As I look back, I can now see that as I was going through this phase of learning my way forward, with the goal of trying to feel better, it was my self-talk, belief system, and mindset that were keeping me trapped in emotional turmoil and unwanted behaviours. Just like when I was super-focussed on my emotional reactions not getting the best of me (and sending me careening down the toboggan hill), there was also a series of changing mindsets that needed to first be discovered (self-awareness) and then dismantled and replaced by healthier coping strategies.

See, I knew it all along!! When I said to my therapist that I was there to pick up just a few new coping skills and then I would be on my merry way, I was right! The surprise was that the old coping skills had to be examined and dismantled first—and that took a bit longer.

SECTION 4

Grow Your Resilience— It's Already Happening

Learning from My Resilience Tree

Resilience is our ability to recover from difficulties—whatever the source of the difficulty might be. The experts tell us that we can learn how to grow our level of resiliency—which is good news! Each of us already has some level of resilience—and it's probably been growing over time depending on a wide variety of factors within our lives.

To better explain what resiliency is, here are a couple of simple scenarios.

If a person were to not get selected for a new job and they had a low level of resiliency, they might react by feeling dejected and convinced that they'll never get hired for any job ever again. That hopeless mindset might remain for days or weeks or months, making them reluctant to apply for any other new jobs.

On the other hand, if that person had a high level of resiliency, they would take the feedback gained from the interview experience, consider what, if anything, they needed to improve in their skillset or resumé, and start looking for other jobs to apply for right away.

Most of us fall in between those two ends of the resiliency scale.

> "Resiliency determines how much something hurts us emotionally, how we respond to that emotional pain, and for how long it hurts."

Our resilience is tested in an infinite number of ways, whether it be a financial setback, a relationship loss, a disappointing weekend, a mean comment from a friend or co-worker, or even a bad hair day. Resiliency determines how much something hurts us emotionally, how we respond to that emotional pain, and for how long it hurts.

I believe that many of us may have a great degree of resiliency in one aspect of our life (for example, our career or social life) but may have a debilitatingly low degree of resiliency in some other aspect of our life (such as our family relationships or whatever else we find challenging to feel secure about).

Having a greater degree of resiliency goes along with having a greater degree of optimism or hope that we'll be okay again one day soon—which keeps us striving forward toward those better days.

Nothing says it better than my resilience tree. This tree is on a very small rocky island across from the cottage we visit every summer. At first, we'd all laugh at its funny shape and wonder if it'd still be there the next year. We've been visiting for over twenty years, and it has been there waiting for us every year—with its various tree branches telling the story of what the past few seasons have been like.

Take a look at it. Isn't it beautiful in its own special way? Has life always been easy for this tree? Were there a few seasons when it wasn't sure it would last? Yet it did! It has continued to sprout a few new branches almost every spring—sticking out at the top in all directions—which adds to its unique beauty. It keeps striving skyward (leaning forward) toward new growth—and it's working.

So, how do we get more of that resiliency? Think of how reassuring it would be to know we could get through whatever life throws at us.

You're already doing that to some extent. It's equally important to consider what you're currently doing that works for you—what helps you to feel more hopeful and ready for life—as it is to consider what you can do to build your resiliency even more. We will do a bit of both as we continue forward on this topic.

"Resilience is a muscle. Flex it enough and it will take less effort to get over the emotional punches each time."

ALECIA MOORE

What the Experts Say

Similar to my earlier suggestion to be prepared to try three different therapists in order to find the person most suited for you, I also suggest that you open yourself up to try a wide variety of resiliency practices to see what feels right for you.

In my various readings, I've come across a wide range of practices. Gratitude, compassion, connection with others, contribution to a cause, and mindfulness meditation, plus many more, are recommended as resiliency practice depending on the research or article you are reading.

One of my favourites is Rachel Thibeault's 5 C's of Resilience. It's probably a favourite because I know and admire Rachel and her work. She refers to:

- ✓ **Centring** (activities that release pent-up energy, anxiety) [which I believe can also foster calm and ground us in our bodies]
- ✓ **Contemplation** (activities that foster mindfulness) [which I believe can help us to reframe our mindsets]
- ✓ **Creation** (activities that allow us to create goodness and beauty) [which I believe includes exploration, play, and all versions of creative activities]
- ✓ **Contribution** (giving back)
- ✓ **Connectedness** (feeling authentic connections with others and with life)[2]

---

2   Rachel Thibeault, "Unsung Heroes: Occupational Gifts for a Meaningful Life," *Spirituality and Occupational Therapy*, edited by Mary Ann McColl (Ottawa, ON: CAOT Press, 2011).

Another favourite is offered by Hugh van Cuylenburg, founder of The Resilience Project program in 2011, and author of a book by the same name (2019). His findings, backed up by research, state that resilience and happiness are based on the three pillars of:

- ✓ **Gratitude** (appreciating what we have rather than focussing on what we lack)
- ✓ **Empathy** (trying to understand another person's feelings, experiences, and perspectives)
- ✓ **Mindfulness** (being calm, rather than irritated, and present in the current moment, rather than thinking about the past or future)

Hmmm, that is a lot to consider. So, where to start?

In my opinion, you need to be in the right mindset to even start thinking about these types of intentional practices. Each of us needs to decide for ourselves when the time is right—and that can change day by day. Just because I focus on a gratitude journal today doesn't mean I'll be in the right mindset for it tomorrow. If the fire is still raging, then please look after your immediate needs. Like I said before, be kind to yourself—I have faith that you know what you need to do and when to do it.

> "Positive coping practices from early in your wellness journey are building blocks for future resiliency. You've already been building resiliency a bit at a time just by finding ways to get through the tough days."

Besides, I've found that many of the coping practices I used earlier in my journey, back when I was feeling the struggle much more acutely, turned out to be building blocks for future resiliency practices. So, in fact, you've already been building resiliency a bit at a time just by finding ways to get through the tough days.

It's All Gonna Be Okay

I worked closely with a friend a few years back. He used to carry his yoga mat, strapped to his carry-on, whenever he travelled for business. Yoga was an important part of his wellness. But then, life took a turn, and he temporarily found himself in a difficult time. When asked if he was still doing his yoga, he replied that he wasn't in the right mindset—at that time in his journey, "the house was on fire," which meant that tending the vegetable garden was not going to be helpful; he had to call the fire brigade.

As mentioned, it's also wise to consider what you're already doing to promote your wellness and resiliency. As you read through the above lists, what jumps out as an easy win because it feels right? For example, if you've already discovered the value of looking at the glass half full (gratitude), be pleased with yourself and think of it as low-hanging fruit. You already have that tendency (at least some of the time), so it'll be easy to nurture the value of it by intentionally noticing whenever you do it and attempting to soak in those good feelings a bit longer than you might have in the past.

The opposite is also true. If you find that something on the list brings up uncomfortable thoughts, then respect yourself and back away from it. For me, that would be contribution. As a result of coming from a family of over-the-top volunteers who have lived a lifetime of service to others, I notice I feel inadequate and confused when I consider this practice. My confusion is because I'm never sure if I'm doing enough—as if not doing enough is a shameful act. So, I find that for the sake of my wellness, I don't attempt to build on this attribute. I've convinced myself that in this area of my life, I'll be satisfied with good enough—it isn't an area where it's smart for me to strive to do more.

If none of these appeal to you, then flip the page and carry on. It would be a disservice if this ended up causing you to *should* on yourself. Shoulding on yourself is not healthy. You're in the perfect space for who you are and where you're going. Have faith in that—it's all going to be okay.

"Stop Shoulding on Yourself"

DR. ALBERT ELLIS

Keep this in mind as you hear ideas on how to improve. Build on what comes naturally or on those suggestions that excite you. Or, set it all aside for right now, if that's what feels best, and know that you'll be open to trying out new ideas if and when they feel right for you.

Over the next few mini-chapters, I'll be sharing some five-minute habits and approaches I found helpful. Take the time to notice how you feel about this discussion on resilience building, and be kind to yourself if thinking about your level of resilience results in uncomfortable feelings. For me, in the beginning, thinking about my resiliency brought up feelings of shame (thinking I *should* already have more of it?!) as well as overwhelm (*oh no, not another thing to add to that never-ending to-do list*). It doesn't have to be that way—in fact, it's unhealthy if it feels this way for you.

If you stick with me through these next few mini-chapters, we'll hopefully find reassuring ways to feel good about growing your resilience just a little more every day.

It Happened! Not Sure When or How, but It Happened!

The other day, I was running upstairs, stumbled a bit, and stubbed my toe. I recovered and kept going, saying to myself, "Oops! That could have really hurt. Glad it didn't."

At the top of the stairs, I paused and realized that I was murmuring words of gratitude that I hadn't suffered more than a stubbed toe. That gratitude thinking was different than what I might've been thinking years ago when I was in a more difficult frame of mind. I'd been writing this book earlier that day, revisiting those earlier times, which is probably why it came to mind. I realized that back then, I would've felt much more pain with that simple little stumble. And it would've been more likely to grow into a great deal of emotional pain as well.

In those days, I might have felt like no one else in the house noticed or cared that I'd stumbled and hurt myself. I'd have told myself that they never noticed when I was hurting or feeling upset. This would have instantly led to "They don't appreciate how hard I'm trying to do so much for them—and how tired I am—and how much hurt I feel inside of me." Tears would likely have come to my eyes. All that negative thinking might've caused me to become mad (in addition to the sad) that I was so unappreciated. That little stumble might have led to a downward spiral, accentuating the negative undercurrent that often rippled through me.

Instead, on that more recent day—at this point in my wellness journey—I was able to simply say, "Oops! That was close," and carry on.

That is a HUGE change in mindset. That is also an indication of having a certain level of resilience. The ability to demonstrate a level of gratitude ("I'm glad that didn't hurt any more than it did"), rather than distress and negativity, is an indicator and key factor of resilience. I'm not sure when that mindset change occurred, but I'm happy it did.

Of course, resiliency is more accurately linked to our ability to handle challenges and life happenings that are much more impactful than a simple slip going up stairs. I am using this simple example to illustrate what I noticed in my mindset. Fingers crossed that it'll be a long while before I have a bigger, life-altering challenge to test the full extent of my resiliency.

Gratitude is one of the habits that is often prescribed if you wish to grow your resiliency—and I agree it's an important factor. However, practising gratitude might be something that a person finds difficult to maintain through the full twenty-four hours of a day. For some of us, at some points in our lives, there might be some healing or personal growth that needs to occur before gratitude becomes a foundation on which we build our lives. The timing needs to be right.

Many years ago, I wrote in a gratitude journal every night before bed—and it was a really good idea for me to do at that point in my life. It helped me feel calmer before trying to sleep, and it helped me to think about gratitude at other times throughout the day—it was one of my stepping stones. But on its own, it wasn't the whole story. I had to get to the point where I was even willing to think about gratitude at bedtime rather than making a list of all the people who had wronged me that day. To be honest, I probably did a little of both some nights.

If I go back even farther, there was a time when I simply wasn't ready to consider gratitude at all. I needed to heal some aspects of my being before I could consider spending a few minutes of precious time to be intentionally grateful. It would have caused more self-critical shame in me (for being so ungrateful the other twenty-three hours of the day—which I would have labelled as a "bad-girl" trait). This would have challenged my mental wellness rather than helping it grow stronger.

Those were the days when I would sometimes go back to bed after finishing a task or phone conversation. I'd climb in, cover up, and chill for a minute. My anxiety was running pretty high in those days. Getting back into bed allowed me a reward of calmness for finishing something I was extraordinarily anxious about, and it actually helped me to be more effective and efficient in that while lying there in my bed, I made a solid plan for what to do next.

Going back to bed might not appear to be a tool of efficiency at first glance, but some days, that was the most effective way to get through a day when it felt like the sky was falling. I didn't spend a long time there (think of it like a smoke break), and it wasn't every day or every task—but there were times when that felt like the best place for me to go to think for a few minutes. (One of the benefits of working from a home office.)

As you can see, the timing wasn't right for me to initiate a daily gratitude practice at that point in my life. What was needed was extra care to help me get through each hour of the day. You won't see "Go back to bed after every task" as an entry in a list of resilience-building ideas, but I'd argue that doing what's needed to care for yourself when times are tough is just as important because it lays the groundwork for when you're ready to get back on your toes, leaning forward, and looking for the next stepping stone that'll help to grow your wellness.

I can look back at those times and judge myself as being in pretty bad shape. Or, I can look back at those times and be grateful for having enough resilience to get through it. (Yay for the little bit of resilience that I did have!)

I can also recall and be pleased that my intuition was to be kind to myself and think of myself as being wise enough to know that going back to bed was just another way of giving myself a quick reward for crossing something off the to-do list and a place to go to reset my emotions and plan for the next task. What might be your safe place when you also need a five- or ten-minute emotional regulation break?

Kindness and empathy are vitally important when supporting other people to find their way through life's challenges and possibly make some changes along the way. Yes, empathy is valuable when you offer it to others, but compassion to ourselves is equally, if not more, important. At least it was for me!

To Dramatize or Not to Dramatize— That Is the Question

We all love a good story. Often, the best ones are focussed on the most outrageous things that happen to us. When we retell the story, the more suspense and drama we can build into it, the greater the chances that all attention will be on us—and for many of us, that feels good. "Can you believe it? It's almost too impossible to be true!"

So, what makes a good story to tell about our day-to-day lives? Is it when all is going fine, with only minor bumps in the road that are overcome easily? Or is it when, for no apparent reason, a very rude person insults us, and then we have to wait an extraordinary length of time in a lineup—for lousy service—making us late for something terribly important? Or maybe it's when you're the sickest you've ever been and have to go to the clinic and then the hospital?

Let's chill for a second and look at this through the *you get what you focus on* lens. Let's consider what you wish to emphasize in your day-to-day life.

In one of my pink-chair musings a long time ago, I noticed that if I used stories of how life was unfair or difficult as my primary conversation pieces, then I'd need a never-ending supply of "Poor me, can you believe it?" stories. *Hmmm*, I thought. *Do I want that?* If I continued, my life might become like that colour experiment. I'd constantly need to be on the lookout for poor-me stories. And if I was looking for them, then I'd most definitely find them. And if I found them, then I'd feel the uncomfortable emotions that go along with those experiences. Did I really want to be on the lookout for mad, sad, and fearful situations? Or would I have better days if, instead, I was on the lookout for feel-good opportunities?

A few years ago, I came across an article on resiliency about the work of American researcher and author Barbara Fredrickson and her concept of **micro-moments of positivity**.

A micro-moment is when, for a split second, you notice something wonderful and heart-warming, but instead of giving it a fleeting glance, you intentionally hang onto those good feelings and appreciate that moment. In other words, it's a **feel-good opportunity**—the opposite of a good drama story.

> "A micro-moment of positivity is when you notice something heart-warming and intentionally hang onto the feel-good feelings that it brings."

For example, you're in line to pay at the grocery store, and the cutest little toddler catches your eye. You manage to have five seconds of engaging eye contact before you are tempted to return to your cell phone. Fredrickson suggests that instead of allowing your focus to return to the stress-based thoughts of your busy day, give into the cute moment the toddler is offering you and milk the impact of that micro-moment of endearing eye contact. Whether a game of peek-a-boo is offered or it's simply a staring contest where you wonder what might be going through their adorable little mind, stay with it for a moment longer and enjoy the warm feelings that flow from this feel-good micro-moment. You'll positively impact your emotions and, eventually, your resilience.

You might be wondering why someone else's toddler in the grocery store is considered adorable if you have your own toddler at home. It can be whatever appeals to you.

Personally, I've been noticing birds lately. Not only the bright-red cardinal in my backyard that seems to be chirping "Birdseed, birdseed," hoping we'll refill the feeder, but I also notice on my weekly trip across town that there's a huge flock of no-name birds that all hang out together on one particular hydro wire. (I'm pretty sure the birds have a name, but they're run-of-the-mill birds that don't sport pretty colours to make it easy for me to identify them.) Sometimes, when I drive by, they decide to switch wires and, en masse, they fly up in one choreographed swoop to a neighbouring wire, making me wonder how it is they could be so magically synchronized. It's a small thing, but it's one of the many sights I take the time to notice and smile about. You can see that it doesn't need to be extraordinary to count as a micro-moment—as long as it brings a smile to your face or joy to your heart.

When we talk about micro-moments in our workshops, people speak of their grandchildren or pets and how much joy they bring to them, or they speak of walking in nature and enjoying the beauty of the water or the mountains. Whatever makes your heart happy is a micro-moment of positivity for you and worth nurturing. If you need help finding those moments in the middle of a busy day, keep a supply of pictures of adorable children, pets, or sun on the water on your phone so you can take a two-minute break to nurture the warm feelings that float through you when you spend time with your photos. Better yet, share the happy memory with a friend and tell them about it. It will make you feel better than the sad or mad feelings you experience when you tell, or retell, that poor-me story.

> "'Positive emotions transform us for the better.' Barbara Fredrickson"

Barbara Fredrickson sums it up by saying, "Positive emotions transform us for the better. If we increase our daily diet of positive emotions, we become better, stronger, more resilient, more socially connected versions of ourselves." (Remember those brain neurons, lining up to create well-manicured paths.)

It's a win–win! Not only is it a good resiliency practice that will impact our ability to overcome the hurdles that invariably come our way, but it's also a pleasant and enjoyable way to move through our days.

So, back to the original question: To dramatize or not to dramatize? Maybe you do need to share with your friend (or better yet, your therapist) an unbelievably frustrating or scary experience every now and then because you need emotional support. Or you may need to do it to heal or to feel connected. But maybe, like I was, you're sharing these stories for conversational reasons. That's when you need to ask yourself: Is this what I want to keep my focus on?

Choosing to minimize the impact of your day's frustrations by actively looking for micro-moments of positivity can encourage more calming, satisfying, and joyful emotions. Louise Hay would tell us that each happier thought is like a drop of water. At first, a few drops of water are barely noticeable, but if the drops keep coming, they'll add up. Soon, you'll have a small puddle, then a larger puddle and, eventually, a beautiful brook flowing around rocks and under shady trees with chirping birds—and that image is worthy of its own micro-moment.

Life Is an Interconnected ~~Mess~~ Creation

I was inspired a couple of years ago by Jason.

I was facilitating a workshop and talking about the value of self-care and its impact on our mental health and resiliency. We were doing an exercise that encouraged participants to look at various aspects of their self-care and to consider which area they might wish to enhance. These included categories such as physical self-care (exercise, nutrition, health), spiritual self-care (being in nature, cherishing hope, taking time for reflection), and emotional self-care (having fun, being pleased with yourself, identifying what feels comforting), plus a few others.

While the others were in table discussions, Jason shared with me how this exercise reminded him of his recent wellness journey. For him, each of these self-care categories seemed to flow from one to the other with miraculous results. Over the last few years, he had lost a great deal of weight (over 100 pounds), in part due to his determination to improve his nutrition and level of exercise. The details of what he had accomplished in lifestyle change were quite amazing—not only did he develop a more slender frame, but also better sleep habits, improved health outcomes, and a more joyful outlook.

He was very clear that while it started with a weight loss goal, it became more than just a physical endeavour. He found that as he focussed on his physical self, he spent more time in nature exercising. Being in nature then led him to spend more time in self-reflection and appreciating nature's beauty. This had a big impact on his attitude and his sense of hopefulness—he began to believe that a better future was possible. He cherished this feeling of hopefulness. He also came to cherish having fun and laughing and spending time with those who truly mattered to him, which boosted his emotional and social self.

He told me he didn't set out to accomplish these self-care categories one after the other. In fact, in the beginning, spiritual and emotional self-care weren't even on his radar. But as he experienced success with his physical well-being, he began noticing his spiritual self-care needs and, eventually, his emotional needs. The process continued to flow forward, bringing new self-care goals and benefits into his awareness.

The process of change had taken on a life of its own. It became clear to Jason that life can't really be divided into succinct categories, but rather, it's all interconnected. Many researchers and thought leaders try to make sense of our world by listing and categorizing (I do this, too), but, in reality, nothing stands alone. We're an interconnected creation of experiences, thoughts, and beliefs—each of us is an amazingly intricate and awe-inspiring creation, as unique and impressive as a snowflake.

Science tells us that the cells of our bodies are constantly being replaced by new cells. Consider the dry skin that flakes off your body. It doesn't mean that you have less skin. Old, dry skin cells are replaced by fresh, new cells. This doesn't just happen with your outer skin. It happens throughout your entire body and brain.

It's also known that the environment inside our bodies will determine the health of related cells. If cells are in a stressful environment (for example, if lung cells are exposed to noxious gases), then there's a risk they won't be as healthy and sustainable as those in a more nurturing atmosphere. For example, if a person were to quit smoking (therefore removing cigarette smoke from their lungs), over time, damaged lung cells would regenerate, eventually resulting in healthier lungs. Those lungs may still have some nicotine damage, but they're a whole lot healthier than they were before. The benefits don't stop there: the health of our lungs impacts the health of our heart and almost every other part of our body.

This got me thinking about those times when I was totally stressed out, mad, and/or sad, when it felt like my entire body was shaking and clenched like a tight fist. All those cells that just happened to be newly created during these periods weren't going to be the healthiest and happiest of my cells, wherever they might be in my body.

Think of how stress can keep your neck muscles tight, your heart pounding, and your thoughts racing. Then, consider how a sense of complete relaxation might ease the ache in your muscles, calm your heart rate, and smooth out your thoughts. If cells are being created every moment, the cells created during a period of relative calm would be much happier and healthier than those created during a stressed-out state. (Yes, I can actually visualize little happy faces, or mad faces, on my trillion-plus cells.)

As each one of those healthier cells comes to life, they'll be impacting other cells in our bodies. It's kind of like a crowd of people. If there's a bunch of happy and kind people in the crowd, rather than a collection of miserable and mean people, the whole crowd will feel the difference. We all rub off on each other.

> "The cells of our body are constantly being replaced. Those created during a period of calm will be healthier."

There's nothing I can do now about those cells that developed during my miserable days, but maybe today, in these five minutes, I can focus on gently relaxing and calming my body so the cells coming to life right now stand a better chance. Wouldn't it be cool if, eventually, the happy, calm, healthy new cells outnumbered the unfortunate cells? It makes me (and my cells) smile and feel more hopeful.

In her video, *Positive Emotions Transform Us*, Barbara Fredrickson adds to this concept by indicating that positive emotions help humans create cells more quickly. This means that giving our bodies and brains a more content environment will result in healthier cells being created at a faster pace. Woo hoo! Happy wins the race!

If you happen to be going down the wrong path right now and are thinking that you're sunk, as you've recently had a lot of miserable and stressful times in your life, don't worry. Remember the first part? Our cells reproduce themselves constantly, over and over again. So, just spend a few minutes right now mindfully trying to be calm and hopeful. Take a big relaxing breath and let your shoulders relax a bit—you're already making a difference.

Oops! Another crisis thought? Oh well, don't worry too much about it. Those cells are going to be replaced at some point in the near future, and you can try again. After all, we're a big, interconnected (sometimes messy) creation—and we get an infinite number of re-dos.

Know Thyself—The Value of Self-Awareness

A few years ago, it became clear that I had a habitual compulsion to find something—anything—to worry about. When there was something worrisome on my mind, it was likely to stick with me nonstop 24/7, even through the night—especially at night—making it challenging to fall asleep.

My worry habit became especially apparent one night when I couldn't calm my mind and get to sleep because I was stressed out about my teenage daughter's former friend. I'd just heard that they were trying to decide if they should stay in university or take some time off from formal education. Really?! I still liked the person and wanted the best for them, but did I have to lie awake that night worrying about the details of their decision regarding continuing education?

> "Self-awareness of our thoughts, self-talk, habits, and emotional state is a key to improving resilience."

I laughed the next morning when I told my husband about it. The good news is that I could find nothing else closer to me to worry about through the night. The bad news is that some nights, my unconscious habit is to find something to worry about, and that isn't helpful to my wellness journey as it's the opposite of a positive resilience practice.

Self-awareness is important. It's informative to know this about myself. I know from experience that it'll take some time to change this worry habit of mine—the change process doesn't work overnight—but I also know that change *does* happen as my neurology gets rewired. If I'm aware of what I don't want for myself and kindly, but persistently, talk myself through the logic of it being an unhelpful thing to do, then it will bit by bit become easier to find my way around it. Self-awareness of our thoughts, self-talk, unfortunate habits, and emotional state is another key to improving resilience.

Having the light bulb in my brain suddenly turn on that night and become aware that I was worrying about someone who was no longer in my sphere of concern was illuminating. Since then, I'll often chuckle to myself and wonder if I'm scratching at the bottom of the barrel for worry material—or if the topic at hand is in fact a legitimate thing to ponder. (As if worrying about something is ever helpful?!)

That little tidbit that I now know about myself has helped me to talk myself through other times when I could feel myself going down that path. Becoming more self-aware about whatever trap it is that you find yourself too easily falling into is an example of that huge leap between step one (precontemplation) and step 2 (contemplation) of Dr. P's stages of change. In my experience, it's challenging to improve something if you aren't aware of what's (unconsciously) holding you back.

Speaking of irrational bedtime worries, we have a family story that we'll sometimes remind each other of as needed. Years ago, while on a family vacation, we were driving late at night, after three fun-packed days at Disney World, toward our next stop, which was a hotel on the beach. It was then that Melissa, our middle child, realized that the beach was on an ocean, and for her, that was terrifying because there were sharks in the ocean. In her overtired mind, that extrapolated to mean that we were (potentially) going to be eaten by sharks the next day.

All four of us other family members attempted to explain to her that it was safe to play in the shallow water of the beach—but with no luck. Her logic had left her, and fear was driving—she continued to be terrified and beyond logic. The next morning, after a restful night of sleep, Melissa had no problem whatsoever and had a great time playing on the beach.

It's a common phrase to say that everything looks brighter in the morning, but for our family, we have a memorable example demonstrating to us that a worry can be extraordinarily scary late at night, yet easy to overcome in the morning. I'll still calm myself every now and then by labelling a late-night worry as a Melissa shark story, and convince myself to wait till morning to evaluate the true risk that's being faced.

Knowing ourselves and being aware of some of the traps we unknowingly set for ourselves can be healthy and helpful. For me, knowing I have a tendency to find something worrisome to think about as bedtime gets closer means that my self-awareness is improving and, therefore, I'm better at noticing it and calling it out for what it is.

I also made adjustments to my bedtime routine once I became self-aware of this tendency. I now take care to not spark any unwanted thoughts before going to bed. Instead, I watch or read something lighthearted that's more likely to make me smile or laugh. If, on some nights, a worrying thought still finds me, I attempt to chuckle about the timing of it, reframe it (if I can), and do my best to let it go until morning, when I'll be in better shape to think about it more clearly.

Contemplation as a Sleep Aid

I have heard that during nighttime, while you're sleeping, your mind naturally processes all the happenings of the day. That's one of the reasons why a good night's sleep is healthy for us and our resiliency.

However, there are times when a good night's sleep is very difficult to achieve. Coincidentally, the nights when we're in our most desperate need of a healthy, restorative sleep are too often the nights when it can be difficult to fall asleep, and when we do, we might wake in the night with the mind still churning.

I eventually learned that, for me, one way to pre-empt a sleepless night is by taking the time prior to bedtime to nurture my stressed-out self by taking a long walk or sitting in my favourite chair, thinking. Thinking can be such a simple and misunderstood word. When I use it here in this context, I'm speaking of taking the time to be with my thoughts and problems, considering them from every conceivable angle and, in the end, trying on different perspectives to see what feels most aligned with who I am and want to be—all the while trying to be compassionate to myself and whoever else might be a part of my thoughts.

Basically, I am determining if I can survive through the challenge at hand, which, in turn, counteracts my body's instinct to go into fight / flight / freeze mode. I try to determine how difficult or dangerous a certain situation is for me. Am I worrying about something that isn't really a big deal, or is it a symptom of something concerning?

This approach fits into Dr. Thibeault's resiliency recommendation of contemplation. It also fits into the concept of mindfulness as I strive to sit with my thoughts and emotions and calm myself into knowing that in the grand scheme of things, it's all gonna be okay.

The situations might be significant some days, but other times, I don't even notice how much something might be bothering me until I'm in the quiet of night, and the thoughts and emotions come back to me for one more visit.

An example might be a stinging comment by a family member or work associate. I had let it pass at the time (to the best of my ability), but it might revisit, and I'd go into full-fledged fear that it was a comment that was an indication of something much bigger. Part of my contemplation would lead me to consider if it was, in fact, hinting at danger *(my reputation or respect was in danger)* or did they say it because **they** were having a bad day (and it was therefore not as big a deal as I was making it out to be)? Or was it a somewhat justified comment that I should take as constructive criticism? Was it an indication the two of us had different opinions or approaches (which may be frustrating but acceptable)? Or was it an indication that the other person had lost trust in me and my way of doing things? And the bottom line always was, "Could I be okay if that was what they meant"? (Do you now see what I mean by looking at something from every possible perspective?)

Over time, I have become quite good at accepting that there are things that happen in my day that I need to think through and analyze in this manner. Learning that this can help me to calmly sort out life's challenges and feel secure (as well as help me to sleep) is valuable.

I've also gotten very good at doing it on the fly—without the painful late-night thinking moments in my chair. In other words, I'm getting more resilient by getting better at emotional regulation.

You might be thinking, *Why do you need all of that thinking time? Just ask them what they meant.* Yes, of course, that's a good option, and it might be the best approach for you. But for someone like me, who's often overly sensitive (especially when I am already in a difficult space), the first consideration was to attempt to better understand if there was anything to ask about. And if there was, I knew I would handle it better if I could think through what to ask, how to ask, and a range of options for how I might respond. For me, speaking up off the cuff might end up giving my emotions free rein to drive my reactions, and that isn't always a good idea. (Note: be cautious around toboggan hills.)

Of course, it's unlikely that any of us could figure out with certainty what's going on in another person's mind, but thinking this through with as much kindness, understanding, and objectivity as possible can help to overcome the sting or fear that the original conversation causes. In turn, when I went to bed that evening, there would be a greater chance that I could fall asleep and let my sleeping mind calmly process the remainder of the day. Not a guarantee that I'd peacefully fall asleep, but most times, it would help. Zzzzz . . .

> Incidentally, have you noticed yet that not only is contemplation a resilience builder, but it's also the second stage in Prochaska and DeClemente's stages of change? Contemplation, which by definition is the practice of observation, examination, and deliberation, is a significant step in getting ready to make a change. In phase one, the precontemplation phase, us humans aren't even thinking about the possibility of changing something in our lives. It's phase two when we contemplate (observe, examine, and deliberate) if it's logical to want to adjust something about ourselves.
>
> Yes! Using contemplation as a resilience booster results in change.

Grounding Yourself in the Present Moment

When I do a peer support workshop, I often begin with a discussion on what participants can do to help themselves if they become emotionally upset by a discussion. It's not that I expect folks to be triggered, but it's a good idea to remind people that they have strategies just in case they need them if a difficult topic comes forward.

If a person is triggered (meaning that their body and mind are reacting because they are involuntarily focussed on a disturbing memory from a different time and place), it can be helpful for them to bring themselves back to the current moment (and away from the recollection and influence of a past trauma). **Grounding** is the term used to describe the practice of bringing your thoughts and emotions back to the here and now.

In my opinion, grounding yourself can also be used as a mini-meditation.

Many people use breathing exercises to ground themselves and bring themselves back to the current moment, or more specifically, to the current inhale or exhale that's happening within their body. If that's your habit, keep it up, as it's helping you and your mental wellness in a variety of ways.

I wish to share another example of a grounding exercise. Give it a try if you wish, and see if it appeals to you. The ideal is to sit in a chair, with your feet on the ground, as you peacefully read through the following.

Begin by thinking about your feet—the soles of your feet . . . As you focus on the soles of your feet, you might be able to feel *them, possibly the arches of your feet. Do they seem to be tingling just a bit?*

Next, focus on the socks covering your feet . . . Sit with that for a moment, then think about the shoes you're wearing . . . the insides of those shoes that are touching your socked feet through to the outside soles of your shoes. Now, can you imagine the carpeting or flooring that your shoes are resting on?

Take your focus farther down, through the carpeting or tile to the floorboards . . . and now through the lower levels of your building. Take the time to feel the connection with the soles of your feet at each stage. Can you feel it? . . . Sit with that for a bit.

Continue focussing down through to the ground below . . . through the various layers of earth that take us to the depths of our earth. Know that you are connected to that ground . . . from the soles of your feet on down to the earth below.

As you read through that imagining, does it bring you a sense of stillness and calm—possibly a grounding to the time and space of where you are in this moment? Even if there are significant concerns from the past and worries about the future, in those few moments while you were reading, you truly were okay—and, hopefully, your body and mind also felt a bit more calm and secure (rather than super-stressed). Each time you find a way to calm yourself, whether it's using this exercise or something

> "Each time you find a way to calm yourself, you're leaning in the direction of mindfulness and practising your resiliency."

else, you're leaning in the direction of mindfulness and practising your resiliency.

I like this exercise because you can do it anywhere, even in a crowded room, without anyone else being aware. If you feel like you need a mini-break from the stressors within you, bring yourself back to this moment and think about the soles of your feet and find your way through to feeling them connecting with the earth below.

It was a veteran participating in one of our courses who first introduced me to this exercise. As he led us through it, we could also hear the quiet snoring of his service dog lying beside him at his feet—which definitely helped us all feel calmer.

Another common exercise to bring you into the present moment is to consider your five senses. Mindfully think about what you're smelling in this moment, what you're hearing in this present moment, what you're tasting, seeing, and what you feel touching your skin or hands in this present moment.

It takes a fair amount of mind control to harness your attention and bring your focus to the mundane experiences of smell, hearing, taste, sight, and touch, but when you do it successfully, you can pull your thoughts into the current moment and away from disturbing memories or future worries. You are almost guaranteed to discover you are safe in that moment. Moment by moment—that's how we live life.

You might even find some satisfaction or appreciation with what you are hearing, tasting, smelling, etc. Can you morph this into a micro-moment of appreciation? If you can, nurture the feel-good moments that come to your attention—and if they don't come forward easily, that's okay, too. Just go back to feeling the soles of your feet on the ground. Know that, in this moment, you are okay and connected to the ground below you.

Mindfully Growing Your Resilience

> "Mindfulness is simply being aware of what is
> happening right now without wishing it were different;
> Enjoying the pleasant without holding on
> when it changes (which it will);
> Being with the unpleasant without fearing it
> will always be this way (which it won't)."
>
> JAMES BARAZ

I'm not as eloquent with words as James, but I find myself saying something similar about my golf game. When I have a good game going, my thought is to enjoy it while it lasts because I know it won't be that way forever. And the same is true when my skill seems to disappear: "Don't worry, it won't last forever. The good shots will return sometime soon."

This also reminds me of those times when I had my days-long debilitating headaches and when I finally decided to stop fighting them and instead give in and simply be with the pain while I patiently waited for it to flow out through that imaginary chute in the top of my head. I was being mindful, according to Baraz's definition.

This may be hard to apply to the rest of our lives, but there's a lesson in here somewhere. Golf, for example, is much more enjoyable when you don't get all tied up in knots because it's not going well—the same might be true about our day-to-day lives.

Having this kind of mindful mindset could be an indicator of resilience. So, I could conclude that my emotional resilience is fairly strong when I golf. (I have not yet lay down and cried in the middle of a fairway because my ball went into the water. My golf resilience allows me to grumble for a bit and then move on and try again.) Thankfully, I'm getting better at approaching the rest of life in a similar manner, but the reality is that I still have some resiliency gaps—areas of my life that can flatten me pretty quickly. There are still areas to work on. The reality is that there'll always be work to do before any of us can say that we have this mastered across all aspects of our lives.

If we let them, our thoughts can take us to moments where mindfulness is necessary to pull us back into calm. Have you ever noticed that when you think about past events that were extraordinarily difficult or upsetting, your emotions and body react as if you were back in that moment? You reexperience the same difficult emotions, your muscles tighten, and your inner voice becomes afraid and negative. Yet, in this moment, you are not *in* that predicament; you're only thinking about it.

> "Mindfulness is intentionally being in the present moment with loving kindness and without any judgment. Just openness and patience for whatever this moment brings."

The same is true looking forward. If we're suffering in this moment because we're worrying about something that hasn't yet occurred (and in many cases, may never occur), then we're calling up difficult and debilitating emotions even though they aren't actually happening right now. Mindfulness and/or grounding ourselves is one pathway out of those uncomfortable moments.

The bottom line is that mindfulness is intentionally being in the present moment with loving kindness (for yourself and others) and without any judgment (of yourself or others). Just openness and patience for whatever this moment brings. *It's easy to write out the definition, much more challenging to accomplish it, but a very worthwhile skill to practice.*

As I look back at the various techniques discussed in Section 3, I can see that I managed to create these mindful moments as I was learning my way through life by listening to my body, considering what I *really* wanted, and intentionally focussing on "This little light of mine." Those are some of the approaches that made sense to me and that I felt were playing a role in helping me feel better day by day.

Little did I know that I was already doing mindfulness practices! Chances are that you also have a few unacknowledged mindfulness practices. Take note of what they are and nurture them. They'll encourage you to grow your repertoire and experiment with others.

Meditation—Kim Style

Meditation seems to be one of the more frequently mentioned strategies for strengthening your feel-good brain matter. It seems to show up in many of the discussions that talk about the neuroscience of resiliency.

But really, what is it, and what is the right way to meditate? For me, that was one of my biggest roadblocks—being concerned about doing meditation correctly. Being a self-conscious perfectionist, I found it very difficult to calm my mind and just be in the moment. Instead, my mind would be buzzing with thoughts about how to breathe, how to sit, what to focus on, and many other stress-inducing thoughts at the very time that I was attempting to do the thing that is all about reducing stress.

Over time, I came to realize that there are many different acceptable approaches to meditation, and the right one is the one that works for you. I've listened to a wide variety of guided meditations over the years, and they've been helpful, but what I've noticed is that many of them speak as if they have the magic answer—the correct way to meditate. While that may be confusing at first, in the end, I found it to be helpful as it pointed out to me that there's no specific right and wrong way.

The goal of meditation is to calm your mind so there are no external (busy) thoughts happening, and then to feel the stillness and peaceful wisdom of your inner soul.

Many guided meditations suggest that you focus on your breath calmly going in, out, and through your body. For me, that isn't a good idea as I start to worry about breathing too fast or too slow or not deep enough (again, I seem to be convinced that if there's a way to do it wrong, I'll find it). Therefore, I don't intentionally think about my breath, but I still notice that my body often takes a cleansing big breath as I start to relax—so it must be intricately connected.

My personal approach to meditation is to focus on fully relaxing all my muscles. Quite often, sleep meditations will help you to do a body scan and work from the top of your head down to the bottom of your feet, gently suggesting that each muscle relax as your thoughts pass over it. I do this while sitting, and it feels glorious to let every single cell of my body relax into a feeling of bliss. I love to sit with this feeling for a few moments. When you feel that sense of blissfulness, you know you must be doing something right.

As much as I love the feeling, it can still be tough some days to harness my thoughts and bring them calmly to my inner body. If my thoughts are out there, bouncing from one item to the next (or super-focussed on a problem to be resolved), then my muscles and mind are not going to easily cooperate.

If the above sounds next to impossible for you to achieve or to even want to try, then set it aside—it might not be right for you. I believe there's more than one way to achieve similar benefits. In my opinion, there are a wide variety of meditative activities available to us—and each of us unique people has our own unique list. Likely, you are already enjoying one or two that are good for you.

That first yoga teacher that I met suggested going for a walk where you drew your breath in for four steps then let it out slowly for the next four steps. You need to think about this if you want to keep it up—so it takes focus. If you try it, you might notice that you end up crossing a lot of ground without realizing it, and you feel more relaxed afterwards since you've given your brain a break. Or you could do yoga! That nap at the end of yoga, in my opinion, is a form of meditation.

Still too intentional or woo-woo for you? Then go out to nature. What's it like when you go fishing or for a walk in the woods? If you're silent, on your own, and noticing that your thoughts are calmly drifting down the river along with the ripples, then you're likely gaining meditative value.

My husband goes to his shop in the basement and builds something. This is great for both of us as I end up getting a new shelf or side table out of it, but more importantly, it's a great way for him to clear his head of the normal day-to-day thoughts and challenges. He gets his mental break from thinking about a totally different challenge, such as how to fit this bolt into that tight corner. If he were to come out of his shop distressed and frustrated (and he has some days), then there wasn't any mental wellness happening that time. But most of the time, it works—it's just what he needed.

I don't think that power tools and building furniture could be classified as meditative (in fact, I'm sure we aren't going to read that anywhere else), but the act of working with one's hands can certainly have meditative qualities. (Remember that creativity showed up on Rachel's 5 C Resilience list?) Do you do needlework or knit, and if so, is it a calming activity for you? When people like you and me are at this point in our journeys, the most important consideration is that each of us finds a way to achieve a mental break that takes us to a feel-good place without any intrusive, worrying thoughts lurking in the corner of our minds.

Meditation is often mentioned by the experts as a foolproof way to build resiliency, so I'll keep trying, but the reality is that there are many hours in the day, and each one of them is important to our mental wellness (not just that half hour or ten minutes of meditation), so keep doing what feels right for you as you lean forward toward discovering other helpful ways to give your mind a break.

Who knows, you may lean forward enough that you find yourself sitting lotus style, with your forefinger and thumb gently poised, and humming, "Aum." Way to go!! So glad you are giving it a try. Let me know if it works for you.

> If you notice your thoughts wandering away from meditative focus and towards external worldly things, gently bring yourself back. Remember that a meditation yogi would not meanly reprimand you if your mind wandered - don't do it to yourself.

It's in the Palm of Your Hands

Years ago, I attended a Women for Women group at my local church with a guest speaker who introduced us to the concept of therapeutic touch. I was impressed to the point of never forgetting. In hindsight, I think it was a preliminary introduction to mindfulness and meditation, even though neither of those was a part of my language at that time.

She had us all experiment by rubbing our hands together for about a minute—long enough that our palms started to heat up from the friction. Then we cupped our two hands together, not quite touching, so there was a ball of space between the palms of our hands. Try it! Do you feel a warm ball of energy between the palms of your hands, the size of an extra-squishy tennis ball? Pause for a moment, let your shoulders relax, take a breath, and notice again the feel of that tingly ball of energy in the palm of your hands.

When I first felt it, I thought it was magical. I loved knowing that I was feeling and holding "my" energy. That was "me" and my power tingling around in that imaginary squishy ball of tingling heat. It mesmerized me that I could feel my inside energy on the outside of me—that I could hold it in the palms of my hands—and it felt like something to be savoured and valued. I also found it very calming.

(Too woo-woo for you? Okay, maybe not an actual ball of energy, but play along and see if thinking about trying to feel the palms of your hands—for at least thirty seconds or so—makes them start to tingle just a bit and brings you a sense of calmness.)

I also discovered I could do it anywhere. I didn't need to necessarily rub my hands together once I knew the feeling I was searching for, so I'd hold my hands gently together whenever I had a moment of quiet or stillness, such as at my children's musical concerts while I was sitting quietly, listening to them play or sing. Or I'd position my hands together at night to calm myself when I was trying to fall asleep. I've even done it with my hands in my lap below a boardroom table when I felt I needed a minute to calm and reset myself. If it appeals to you, try it the next time you're at a tense meeting and need a moment.

This simple little practice became a starting point for experimenting with meditation—and some days, even now, it's a sixty-second replacement for meditation. Personally, I've always felt rushed and like I was going to run out of time, so I have several meditation substitutes that are good enough for when I don't feel like I can fit anything else of more substance into my life.

When you're at a stop light or sitting on the bus, cup your hands together and feel the heat of that imaginary ball of energy between your palms. Or, take a big breath and, when you let it out, attempt to feel the muscles in your head, neck, and shoulders relax. Take another breath and feel even more muscles relax. If there's time for a third breath, relax even more (but be sure to keep one eye open so you notice when the light turns green).

> "Gently cup your hands together and focus on feeling the heat of that imaginary ball of energy between your palms."

Or when you're taking a walk—possibly with the dog or on your way to the office—notice your breath and take a long breath in for four steps and then out for four steps. Or make it three steps, if that suits you better. As you breathe in for those steps, you may wish to think of a subtle string gently pulling the lower part of your ribs forward, matching your forward walking pace.

Or, better yet, think about that inner light within you, resting between your lower ribs in your sacral chakra, and with each breath in think about how you're drawing air toward that flickering candle that's your inner light, oxygenizing the glow. You could even hum, "This little light of mine, I'm gonna let it shine."

I've been successful enough with meditation to know that I love the tingly feeling that comes with full relaxation. And I fully believe in its health benefits. It seems obvious to me that it's having a positive influence on my heart and circulatory system and all the other systems within my body. Personally, I believe there can be detrimental damage to our internal systems, especially our musculoskeletal system, if our bodies are experiencing constant anxiety and stress. So the reverse must be true when we find a way to bliss out into a complete relaxation of our minds and bodies, even if it's only for a few minutes.

Feeling our energy like this reminds me of how we all rub off on one another. I know you've noticed, at some point in your past, how one person in a foul mood can rub off on others around them, and suddenly, you have two or three others also grumbling. Hopefully, you've also experienced the feel-good energy of a person who joins a conversation and, suddenly, others in the group are also feeling more jovial or optimistic.

I visualize this (in my woo-woo mind) as each of us rubbing shoulders with others around us. As we work together, live together, or play together, our emotional energy will rub off on others around us. It happens whether we think about it or not, but if we were to give it a bit of thought, we may choose to be a little more picky about who we hang around with—as well as considering what kind of energy we wish to put out there into our own day-to-day activities.

Remember back when I suggested that before getting out of bed in the morning, you might want to call forward three descriptors of what you would like for yourself for that day, such as calmness, confidence, and clarity? This same exercise can be dusted off and used again prior to going to a meeting, party, or family event, with you deciding which type of energy you would like to take with you as you go forward toward rubbing shoulders with others. Possibly, you could call forward optimism and creativity as you walk down the hall to go to a work meeting, or gratitude and loving-kindness on the drive to a dinner celebration with the extended family.

Whether we realize it or not, we all give off gentle ripples as we enter a space, as if we were a pebble being dropped into a pond, so think ahead as to what hue of ripples you would like to contribute. If for no other reason than it will be a good resiliency practice that in the end will benefit you the most.

> Visualization, imagination, mindfulness, and intention are all suggested in this one chapter!! So, really, does this kind of woo-woo work?
>
> David Hamilton wrote a book on that very subject, *Why Woo-Woo Works: The Surprising Science Behind Meditation, Reiki, Crystals and Other Alternative Practices*. In my opinion, we don't really need science to prove it when we are already feeling like it is helpful. But it sure did make me feel better to see that a researcher could collect enough (respected) research to demonstrate that there is, in fact, a mind-body connection. Thank you, Dr. Hamilton, for calming my mind on that one!

There's More than One Way to Live Life

I love my mom. I always have, and I always will. She has been there for me, supporting me for my entire life—and these days, I'm blessed to be able to take my turn and be there for her.

Life didn't roll out as planned for my mom. She tells me she dreamed of a lifetime with my father, the love of her life, and being surrounded by a small brood of happy children. It didn't happen that way. Following my father's death, she and I were a team of two that went through the majority of my growing-up years.

Did that slow her down? Yes, of course, significantly for a while, but in time, she found her own way of coping and continuing forward. My mom was (and still is, at times) a force of energy who became involved in and contributed to many community clubs and causes. It seems to me that contribution was one of her primary go-to resiliency builders. That, and fun—lots of social interaction and fun!

In her younger years, if there was a piano nearby and a group of fun-loving family members or friends, then there was a party centred around a singalong of old-time favourites. "You Are My Sunshine," "Don't Fence Me In," "Beer Barrel Polka," and "Mountain Dew" are only some of her repertoire. Of course, new lyrics and suggestive expressions were often intertwined into the fun.

I grew up knowing that my mom's happy place was at the piano, with me tucked into a chair beside it, usually at my aunt and uncle's. At least one other person would be perched on the piano bench beside Mom, and several others would dance in the middle of the room. All would be singing with great exuberance.

I learned a lot about life from those experiences—and in my adult years, I learned that each of us has our own way of coping and having fun.

I'm so grateful that I lived alongside my mom as she thoroughly enjoyed herself. These memories still bring me warm feelings. However, I'm also grateful that I've discovered my own version of coping and having fun—which is different from my mom's.

> "We are all unique people with unique approaches to finding the stepping stones that are best suited for each of us."

As I've said many times, in many ways, we're all unique people with unique approaches to finding the stepping stones that are best suited for each of us. Hopefully, some of my stories and visualizations appeal to you and you give them a try. But more importantly, I hope they spur you forward to discover your own approaches. Whatever works for you is right for you.

How Much "Practice" Does It Take?

I received a call from my dear older friend, Margaret, the other day. She was saying how much she feels alone now that a close friend of hers has moved out of her building. The friend used to be there for short daily visits, and Margaret knew that if she ever needed support, the friend would be there for her and vice versa. Of course, there were other friends in the building—but this friend was special.

Like most of us, Margaret had been through a lifetime of mostly happy times but also with occasions of loss, heartache, and disappointments mixed in over the decades. What she said next was very telling: "Oh well, I will be okay. I've done it before, so I can do it again." That right there is a statement of resilience and an indication of a resilient mindset.

Resilience is something we learn naturally when we experience hardship and come out of it feeling like we survived. It might have been horrible at the time, but we survived, so we know we can do it again. Margaret would have scoffed at me if I had used a fancy term like resilient to describe her, yet she was, in fact, using her memory of past similar experiences and logical reasoning to remind herself that she would be okay. Her strong character and natural pragmatism had pulled her through up until this point, and these traits were continuing to support her now.

Not everyone has these qualities at their disposal. Some folks (like myself, at some points in time) might fall back into dramatizing the terrible story to gain attention or sympathy, or spend excessive time looking through poor-me glasses where we can only recall other times when we have had to survive a disappointment or loss. Margaret has been worried about this for a few weeks—and she's justified to be truly disappointed that her friend is moving away—but in the end, her resilience is showing up to support her as she adjusts to this new reality.

In addition to this process of developing resilience naturally as we experience life, experts and articles refer to a **resilience practice**. In other words, we try out a new activity or thinking process that's believed to help us feel better. We *practice* it by intentionally spending time experimenting with the new activity. Of course, we aren't going to be proficient at something that's new to us, but if it appeals to us, then we can practice it until it becomes a regular thing. Eventually, it'll become a habit.

And . . . the more we practice something, the likelier it is that the neurons firing together in our brain will wire together, making it that much easier and more of a habitual reflex to actually respond in a more resilient manner—kind of like a frequently used alternate path down a toboggan hill.

The change model applies here as well, even though you aren't necessarily trying to change an old habit, but rather simply wishing to feel better. You begin by (possibly) not even having the intentional practice of resiliency on your radar . . . until you get to the point that you start to contemplate if it might be beneficial for you. The list of options to be considered in the planning stage can range from looking for micro-moments of positivity and seeing the glass half full to grounding ourselves through the soles of our feet or the palms of our hands—The Resilience Project's gratitude and mindfulness suggestions.

My advice is to notice what you tend to do naturally and lean into it, as that is your low-hanging fruit—something you're already in the habit of doing. Then add in whatever else

> "Notice the resiliency or calming practices that you tend to do naturally and lean into them, as they are your low-hanging fruit."

seems enticing to you. Possibly start a creative project or join a group of like-minded others as you contribute to a charitable endeavour. (Remember Rachel's 5 C Resiliency Builders: creativity, connectedness, and contribution?)

Above all else, remember that even if you aren't intentionally doing a resilience practice, you can still be growing significantly in your level of resilience. Don't minimize the impact of the various little things that help you manage the negative undercurrent and feel better in the moment. It's all helping you to lean forward toward building on the resiliency you already possess.

Above all else, make sure it feels calming or fun. More tasks on the to-do list aren't what you are looking for!

SECTION 5
Bringing It Home—Forward We Go

Getting Ready to Be Ready to Be Ready . . .

I've been quite open and honest as I wrote this book. I've shared some of my toughest times and several of my goofier ideas—that's not typically what I'm like. Sure, I share some of my personal stories when in a training session or supporting another person, but to put it all out there so everyone and anyone can read it?! That's a big deal for me.

I've been thinking about doing this—sharing my stories and strategies—for quite a few years now, but it took a long time to be *ready* to do it. At first, I was way too insecure about this part of my life. In fact, I hid all my writings and thoughts about this so no one would ever know about this crazy idea of mine that little ol' me might have something to say—let alone write a book.

Then, there was the investment of time it'd take to actually write a book. I've always perceived time as a super-limited resource—way beyond considering my days to be busy. Rather, it was connected to one of those deep-down beliefs that I didn't have enough time to accomplish the day-to-day important stuff (that would make me valuable or important enough to warrant living life), let alone do something so frivolous and ridiculous as *write a book*.

Then, there was the phase I went through where I thought that maybe those who knew me through my mental health and peer support work might appreciate what I had to say, but God help me, there was no way I could let my extended family or friends read these details.

Now, finally, I've decided to be brave and go for it.

As I progressed through those many years—and yes, it took years of changing mindset and growing confidence to get to this point—I'd frequently listen to Abraham and Esther Hicks talking about the "getting ready to be ready to be ready to be ready . . ." process. And it made perfect sense to me! Each time it came up in the various audio messages I'd listen to, I'd think about this book, and I'd be reassured that it was in the process of happening even though there was no apparent indication of it happening at the time. I was in the process of getting ready to be ready. And now, here it is!!

I believe that the "getting ready to be ready . . ." process applies to almost everything. It's kind of like entering school on the first day of kindergarten, knowing it's going to take some preparation (and mindset adjustments) to be ready for post-secondary school.

Revisiting Prochaska and DeClemente's stages of change, there's another, possibly more accurate, way to portray the phases. Way back in Section 2, they were organized into a staircase, but once you get to the top, where do you go next?? It's not like you make some adjustments to your thinking or actions and are then considered *done* and good to go for the rest of your life.

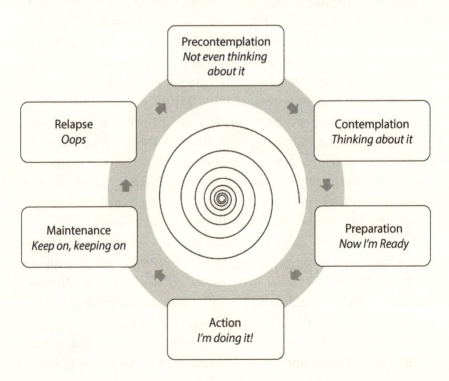

Instead, we're always moving through the spiral of phases—repeatedly, over and over again, with a new goal each time (even though we may not be aware it's happening). And, it becomes a tad easier each time we go through the process since we unconsciously know that we've done it before, so we can do it again. As my colleague, Hayley Peek (who works with me on our Supporting Through Struggle workshop) says, it feels like each of the rings shrinks a bit each time we go around because we know where we're going, which impacts our hope and faith that change WILL happen.

> "We're repeatedly moving through the spiral of change phases, with a new goal each time."

Some days, I think I'm in the final stretch of this personal journey of change, but I'm just fooling myself as I'll be going around those circles on a regular basis, possibly without even realizing it, till the end of my days. At least, I hope I will, since I can now look back and be so grateful that I've already been around the circle more than a few times.

Yucky Days Still Happen

"Wait! What? We are almost at the end of this 'It's All Gonna Be Okay'- themed book, and now you're saying yucky days still happen?!"

Is that what you're saying to yourself?

Sorry, but I need to be honest. Life is still life, and I'm still me. Both life and me come with confusing and messy bits. That's a good thing because life is supposed to be about constant change and adjustments, with a sampling of disappointments and frustration along with the celebrations and joy.

Now that my life has slimmed down to occasional work projects and no children at home, it's so much easier to notice when I'm not myself and to isolate what might be causing it. Or, more importantly, what I might be able to do to get out of the yuckiness.

For me, the yuckiness can take several shapes and styles. Some days it's a sadness that I can't seem to determine the reason for, and other days it's an impatience that turns pretty quickly to anger when things don't go my way.

It happens rarely these days (thankfully), but I still feel the pull of the dark undercurrent of sadness at times. I am now in a space where I can notice it and think, *Isn't that interesting. I wonder why?* In earlier days, I would've been engulfed in it without even knowing that it was lurking nearby. It's still not a pleasant feeling, but I feel more in control knowing that I can approach the feeling in a curious and compassionate manner.

For me, that undercurrent feels like a deep, dark, strong river, just under me, that's trying to take me along into an even deeper and darker place. I can feel it nipping at the edges of my toes and my mind, and if I get too close, it causes me to think from the perspective of, *Why bother trying to feel good? It's too much trouble to try, and besides, what's the point?* It seems like if I were to give up for just a second and fall in, rather than hold myself back from it, I'd get swept up into that ugly current. Those days, when I'm battling to keep myself from falling into the current, aren't easy—but I've learned that loving-kindness and self-compassion help them to pass.

I'm now able to look back and understand more fully why it was so hard at times in years gone by. Fighting that undercurrent, and that thinking, takes a lot of energy and determination. I don't ever remember feeling like it had completely overtaken me for any length of time, but just knowing that it's nipping at your toes and trying to keep yourself above it is hard. If you've experienced those days too, you also deserve a big hug and acknowledgement of how hard it was.

I find that when those days revisit, my instinct is to ask myself, *Why am I feeling this way?* But I've learned the hard way that I can drive myself crazy (*crazier*) by spending too much time trying to figure out the why. I've learned that if the essence of an answer comes to me in those times, then I listen to what my intuition is telling me and honour it. But if nothing comes, I must accept it for what it is and ride the (unwanted) wave of emotion. Sometimes, it just happens without any apparent explanation. Accepting that it happens sometimes—and knowing that it will eventually go away—takes some of the edge off. It's like a super-bad game of golf; it'll eventually get better again. Knowing that doesn't improve my score, but it helps take the edge off.

The other thing that still overcomes me now and then is what I call a **stress hangover**.

All this living and learning, growth and wisdom—and there are still days where I get the shakes, deep down in that space between my chest cavity and my stomach. These are often accompanied by, or following, a severe headache. And often with a feeling of dread and inadequacy.

I might be able to relate it to having just been through a stressful event—even if it was a good, socially fun event or a successful

It's All Gonna Be Okay

work event. I find that I can still end up with that shaky, inadequate feeling.

Oh well, life goes on. The ongoing learning and wisdom help me to realize that these days don't last forever. In the earlier years, I discovered (by negating and pushing myself) that I can live through it and even be functional. So, onwards I go. These days, I soothe myself with the knowledge that the yuckiness will pass—I'm not sure exactly when, but it will pass.

Louise Hay would tell me to do affirmations to help me through this phase. Okay—"I am safe and strong, and life is working out in the best possible manner." And in actuality, that is true. Thank you, life.

Ester and Abraham Hicks would tell me to turn my attention to something else that is good and positive, and not to focus on the problem. I agree! If I repetitively complain about the problem to others, it doesn't make it go away, so I try to be kind to myself, look around me to find something beautiful to focus on, and just *be* with it, knowing that it too will pass.

My psychotherapist would be willing to *be* with me and fully listen to whatever thoughts might come out as I try to make sense of what might be bothering me. I've done that lots of times in my years with him and appreciate all of it. He offered me patience, kindness, and a supportive and safe space in which to explore what might be causing me to feel like this.

And last but not least, my husband asks me when my next doctor's appointment is. "Are you sure you're okay?" he asks with a worried concern for my health. But no, this is just me and the way my body reacts every now and then. If only I knew exactly what it was reacting to.

So, if I can, I'll just take some time to sit still, whether it be with a book, the TV, or a nap. And if I can't do that, I'll carry on with a reminder to go slower, set my expectations for myself a bit lower, and be kind to me. Tomorrow is a new day. Let's see what it brings. This, too, will pass.

Understanding Our Long-Ago Bruises

Like all of us, my upbringing consisted of some hurts. Some big (like my father passing), but most were much smaller and were likely not noticed by anyone else around me (like a silly schoolyard comment that hurt or embarrassed me). Sure, they might have been insignificant (in other people's opinions), but if they hurt me at the time, then they became a part of my makeup.

The time I spent in therapy and with my many self-help books helped to lessen the impact of those hurts, but the leftover bruising may not ever be completely eliminated. The pain is manageable, but it is still there, like a shadow in the corner of me. Every now and then, someone will say something to me that pokes a finger into the middle of a bruise, often without even realizing it.

In years gone by—back near the beginning of this book—I'd be oblivious to the shadow of a long-ago bruise and, without realizing what was happening, would find myself in emotional turmoil, possibly with angry (defensive) words, hot, angry tears, and self-recriminations, probably followed by shame. The full deal might not show up every time, as I was pretty good at coping—but it would be happening inside, and some version of it would come out at some other inopportune time.

As I'd come to a standstill out there in the middle of the field beyond that toboggan hill after one of these reactions, I'd be in too much emotional turmoil to be able to focus with a clear mind about how it all got started. Poking that bruise would trigger much more pain in me. Unfortunately, those bruises—even though they were hidden—were a lot touchier back then.

These days, I'm more aware of the bruises I carry with me, and because I've revisited the sight of the wound and helped my little-girl understandings (and my teenage and young-adult understandings) mature a little, I'm able to keep things in a healthier perspective. *Thank you, Dr. Fowler.* My coping no longer involves covering things up and pretending; rather, these days, I cope by striving to figure out what's really going on inside, honouring it, and then deciding how I wish to go forward.

It is my belief that when any one of us spins out of control into an emotional outburst of mad or sad, it's likely linked to one of our earlier-in-life painful moments. Not all of us have identifiable traumas, and besides, it's not up to anyone else (except for the person who experienced it) to decide if something was traumatic or not. If it hurt you, then it hurt you, and that's all that matters. My personal preference is to not refer to my hurts as traumas—and that's my choice. (You'll make that decision for yourself—whatever language or terminology feels right to you *is* right for you.)

> "When you spin out of control into an emotional outburst of mad or sad, it's likely linked to one of your earlier-in-life painful moments."

Those hurts get buried in the layers of our lives and sometimes don't show up again for decades. This can make it challenging to identify that they're there, but that doesn't stop them from festering in pain and/or becoming a painful bruise. The slightest provocation (warranted or not) can slip through the layers of our lives and poke that pain.

Remember that possibility the next time you find yourself in emotional turmoil. Give that little person inside of you a kind word and loving hug, and know that the more understanding you are with yourself, the greater the chance you'll uncover and begin to heal that long-ago hurt. Now that you have better awareness of what's going on, you can patiently work toward changing your undesirable reactions when a long-ago bruise gets poked.

Remember that it's the same for others as well.

A Lifetime of Unintentional Visualizations

My cousin Dorothy is another of the many angels who have shown up in my life. When I was a young teen, just prior to starting high school, Dorothy and her husband, Wayne, invited me to live with them as a mother's helper during the harvest season on their farm.

Dorothy was mother to a three-year-old and a two-month-old baby, feeding three meals a day to a gang of four farm workers, who lived on cots in the basement, while Wayne spent his waking hours managing the harvest. My role was to help out with whatever I could related to the children, meals, and household chores—and they paid me (which was a first for me)!!

The first summer led into a second and third summer as another baby girl was born into their busy, loving family.

The time I spent with them was a gift to me. I grew up as an only child in a single-parent family, and I was painfully shy, with only a few friends. To be a part of a typical family at that time of my life is something I will value forever. And it allowed me to experience commonplace things that I was not used to, such as Wayne coming in from the fields before dinner and chasing Dorothy (in a fun-loving way) around the kitchen as she was busy doing last-minute meal prep, trying to give her an extra big squeeze of affection. It was such a little thing, but seeing them have fun with their love and affection for each other gave me a memory I have never forgotten.

I can recall sending a Mother's Day card to Dorothy and writing that I hoped that one day I would be lucky enough to have a family just like theirs—with two fun-loving parents and three adorable daughters. Was that a form of (unintentional) vision board or affirmation? Maybe yes, maybe no. Coincidentally, I have my own loving family with three children and have caught myself more than once slipping up and referring to my eldest daughter with the name of Dorothy's eldest. Mind you, to be fair, I've also caught myself calling my son by our dog's name—so it might just be me!

There's a good chance I would've still met my husband and had three children even if I hadn't spent those summers on the farm—that's very likely. But the memories that have popped into my head over the years of my time with them have definitely impacted my family values and worldview.

On a slightly different note, I also recall overhearing my aunt, Dorothy's mom, tell my mom about Dorothy calling to say that she hadn't slept at all the night before because she was so excited about the next day—whether it was Christmas, a birthday, or a vacation trip.

Even as a little girl, I remember thinking it interesting that excitement could be a reason for not sleeping. I can't say why, but it obviously was interesting enough that I remembered it into my forties and fifties as I managed to go through my own sleepless nights.

There are a lot of reasons for being unable to sleep. I'm wise enough to know that my experience isn't the only kind that exists. For me, it often felt like my whole body was on overdrive—my muscles would be tight and unable to relax, my mind would be non-stop and often practising a zillion versions of whatever difficult conversation I thought I might have the next day, and my fears would be over the top, whether it was about a business project, money, or the health and wellness of my loved ones.

And the one constant during those nights was a fear of how I would ever get through the next day if I didn't sleep for the next five hours—nope, still awake, so now it's only four hours—oh no, still awake, I only have two possible hours of sleep.... A resilience lesson I learned during the baby years was that I *could* exist on very little sleep. Telling myself that I could get through the next day just fine, even if I didn't sleep at all, would calm me and take at least that worry off my mind.

Since there's a lot of time to think when you're awake in the middle of the night, I'd recall that memory of Dorothy being too excited to sleep. I thought about how excitement and anxiety are comparable. They're both heightened emotions about something that make it difficult to feel relaxed and calm. By this point in my life, I knew Dorothy well enough to know that it wasn't just excitement for whatever was coming the next day that might keep her awake; I also assumed that she, too, had a few nights of difficult (or non-existent) sleep due to worry and concern.

> "Excitement and anxiety are comparable. Experiment with reframing a middle-of-the-night worry into excitement for possibly overcoming a challenge."

That line of thinking led me to experiment with reframing what I was feeling. Was I super-worried about the next day, or could I label it as excitement for the possibility of overcoming a challenge? I would tell myself that if (and sometimes that felt like a big *if*) the work challenge or difficult conversation worked out to be a good experience (or as good as could be expected), then this would be something to be excited about (rather than nervous about).

Yes, I know that's a long shot (and sometimes not even appropriate), but if my mind was insistent on thinking about it, then I would attempt to reframe it as an excitement for a potentially good outcome.

As you do this and hold on to the possibility of being excited for the accolades or self-pride or relief that will occur, then there is a greater chance of feeling better about it rather than fearful. While that doesn't guarantee sleep, it at least feels better while you need to be awake with it. I remember noticing that my body relaxed just a bit as I turned my thinking in that direction; hopefully, yours will as well.

So, what keeps you stressed out—whether through the night or throughout the day? If you take a look at it from a slightly different angle, could you stretch your perspective and think about it a little differently? More importantly, does that different perspective help you feel a little better—possibly more in control and on your toes, leaning forward, rather than feeling helpless? I hope so—maybe it's worth a try.

I Can Only Be Me

Funny story... during my brief time as a college instructor, I found myself one day talking to eight young-adult students. I had caught them cheating on a group project. Each group of four students was to do part B of an extended project that involved handing in a project plan that included a timeline, with milestone dates, of how they were going to achieve the completion of the project by the due date.

A few days before, as I was reading the many, many plans that were handed in, I came across one that seemed very familiar. The company they were researching was a very common organization that way too many students used, but it was more than that. I had this feeling that I'd read this project plan before. I quickly looked through a stack of past projects from previous terms but couldn't come up with the original. Then, a few hours later, there it was again from another group! Except this time (pardon me for saying so), this group was too lazy to even cheat properly. That was the funny part of this story: they had left the milestone dates unchanged from those used by the original group and the original project. The dates were from two terms before. I thought this was hilarious, and it made my proof of cheating by both groups very easy to prove.

So, the next time we had class, I requested that the eight students stay behind as I wanted to chat with them. As you may know, cheating in a post-secondary program can be grounds for expulsion. I'd decided to deal with this differently and attempt to make it into a teaching moment.

As the eight students faced me, I said to them, "I know that both of your groups cheated on your project submission."

Various explanations were offered, each one beginning with, "No, Miss, we didn't cheat. This is what happened . . ."

With each excuse, I continued to say, "I have a way of knowing for sure that you cheated." (I never did disclose how it was that I knew for sure—that one of them had forgotten to change dates).

We weren't getting anywhere as a group, so I began speaking to them one at a time.

I can't recall much of the details with each of the eight, but there was one young woman who seemed to be sincerely concerned about being in this predicament and attempted to explain her position. One of the several statements that she made was, "There is a lot of schoolwork to do with a full course load with so little time and so much pressure to do well."

> "Each one of us can only be who we truly are. Being the real *you*, rather than striving to be someone else, will lead you to the life that you were meant to live, and you'll thrive in that life."

I sincerely empathized with the pressure that she must be under, and the words that came out of me were something like this, "Each one of us can only be who we truly are. If we think we can do better in life by being someone else, or in this case, using someone else's work, then it won't be real and, in the end, it won't work out well. Be *you*, whether that is an A student or a C student, and that'll be perfect for you. It'll lead you to the life that you were meant to live, and you'll thrive in that life."

I pondered that conversation for a long time, and as you can tell, it still comes back to me now and then. I have no idea where the thoughts came from that day, but they made an impact on me. Hopefully, they also meant something to that young adult and the others with whom I spoke.

These days, I shorten it to a bit of a mantra for myself: "I can only be me. And that is perfect for me!" It's wise advice, and for me, it calms me down to know that the only thing I can do really well is to go forward as who I truly am, rather than trying to be someone or something that I'm not.

A few years ago, I was invited to participate in a large national conference for human resource specialists as an expert. You don't need the details; just trust me as I tell you that it was one of the many times that I walked forward into an opportunity, nervous at times and excited for the challenge at other times. If you had asked my insecure "not good enough" self, you would have heard that a *big* mistake was being made if they thought I was an expert at anything! But forward I went, constantly reminding myself, *I can only be me*. If me wasn't good enough, then fine, I wasn't meant to be there, and that was okay. *Apparently, the me others had gotten to know thought I was well-suited for this, so I'll give it a go.*

The "I can only be me" mantra pops up often and in a lot of different scenarios. Even in social situations with new people, there are times when I want to run and hide. But you know what's always true? I can only be me. I can remember, as a young adult, attempting to be cooler or more sophisticated than I really was, and sometimes I even pulled it off (at least I *think* I fooled them). But it was no fun and really didn't add up to creating friendships that were sustainable.

If people appreciate me, the real me, then it's going to work, and if they don't *get* me, then that friendship isn't meant to happen. If I have an interaction trying to be something I think I *should* be rather than the real me, then it's going to be hard work, it'll likely give me a brutal headache, and it's only a matter a time before I mess it up.

This is basically another story about honouring our true selves and letting the light deep within us shine out as we strive forward to be the person we were meant to be—rather than striving for perfection based on that rule book that's cramping our style.

Kim Sunderland

I can only be me—and you can only be you—and that's perfect for each of us.

"You can fail at what you don't want, so you might as well take a chance at doing what you love."

JIM CARREY

Getting Comfortable with the DEL Key

I did it again this morning. I was writing a fun little chat message to a group of friends, laughing about something I saw in the news. I typed out the sentence, "It's hard to believe that this could ever turn out to be okay." I took a look at it and then backspaced over it to delete it.

Why would I want to put a negative message like that out into the world? At the moment, I wanted to say it because it felt fun and funny, but really, was it? What I really wanted was for that situation that I was writing about to have a good ending. And, if I truly believe that what we say can have an impact on what actually happens (you might want to reread that section on affirmations), then why would I write something negative—even if I thought it was funny?

I know, I know, it's way too out there to believe that our thoughts and words impact the eventual outcome of anything, especially when it's only me—one person—who is taking that concern to heart.

But on the other hand, if everybody related to a challenge took a negative attitude, then that challenge becomes known as hopeless—and if it's hopeless, then don't bother trying. There may be times when we all may want to throw our hands in the air and say, "Forget it. We're never going to get anywhere with this." But if we do that, what are we contributing? Do we wish to contribute to the hopelessness of the problem, or contribute to the hopefulness of *knowing* that a solution will be found? I admire leaders who step up and try something new when faced with social challenges, so why shouldn't I strive to be more like them—at least in what I think or say?

That's what I call an affirmation attitude, and I believe it to be powerful. It's an indicator of my mindset—or better yet, where I'd like my mindset to be on an ongoing basis.

> "If you intentionally contribute to the hopefulness of *knowing* that a solution will be found, you are practicing an affirmation attitude."

Let me get even more personal now. Lately, I've been using my DEL key to keep myself from saying something self-deprecating about myself or my loved ones. Once I started paying attention, I could see that it was something I used to do to protect myself.

I can see now that it used to be a habit to tell others in conversations and emails about my shortcomings, both with and without humour, as a defence tactic. Here's my (screwed-up) logic. It seemed to me that if I let someone know that I was aware of my deficiencies, then I could protect myself from the potential embarrassment of them thinking that I was unaware of how stupid or incapable I was. But, really, what kind of screwed-up thinking is that? I cannot control that you might think I'm deficient, but at least I can control (or pre-empt) any additional judgment that I don't even realize that I'm deficient?

Hmmm! Not enough money in the therapy budget to figure out why I think that way, and this is one of those situations where I don't need to know why. It's enough that I'm aware of this thinking and, therefore, able to start working on finding ways to stop myself from pointing out to others that I'm flawed. Here we go again, up, down and around those stages of change.

The bottom line is that there are a lot of reasons for double-checking what you're typing in those quick messages. Is it consistent with what you really want to put out in our world? Is it helpful to you and your journey? What about being helpful to the person you're communicating with?

And most importantly, if it doesn't feel like it's representing the real you (remember that mantra, I can only be me), then take a step back, use that DEL key, and put your real self out there.

For me, these days, I like it better when I'm around hopeful, leaning-forward people and communities. So, I think twice about what I say and strive to only offer hopeful, positive comments that fit with the positive affirmation attitude that I wish for myself.

Becoming the New You

> "A man who views the world the same at fifty as he did at twenty has wasted thirty years of his life."
>
> MUHAMMAD ALI

People change. So do relationships. Maybe not all relationships change, but I believe that the majority of them do.

I remember reading, back when I was in the midst of trying to change my thinking and way of being, that in each of our relationships, there is an established way of reacting back and forth with each other.

In other words, you believe you know me based on our past relationship (and I know you), so when I do this, you say that . . . and on it goes in both directions, back and forth. This can be a challenge when we're striving to adjust parts of ourselves, since the other person will unknowingly respond in a way that tries to keep us in the same old patterns of thinking and being.

That's not the other person's fault. It's just an unconscious habit/pattern. We all say and do things that would fit into the pre-established pattern as if each of us were to never grow or change. We all do it to each other because we're human. It's natural.

So, if we feel caught in a relationship pattern, what do we do? What can we do?

I propose that we begin by simply noticing it when it happens and attempt to remain in non-judgment (of ourselves and the other person), saying to ourselves, *Isn't that interesting. There we go again.* The reality is that in the past, you played your role in establishing this pattern—no one person is fully to blame.

The other thing to do is to double down on playing your new role. As much as you can, continue to think, be, and respond in the manner you wish for yourself. (Of course, you'll slip up at times, but that's okay—it's a natural part of the change process.) Maintain understanding and compassion for yourself—and for the other person—as you strive forward.

I see this happening in my adult children. They've had a way of being with each other over the years, yet as they've grown in wisdom, they have naturally adjusted their values and ways of being. At times, one will unexpectedly jump to a (negative) conclusion based on a long-ago way of being. It's not pretty when that happens—it was never pretty when they felt hurt and/or mad at each other—but the important part is that it happens less frequently now as they're all in the midst of developing new patterns and ways of being with each other.

I've also caught myself attributing a long-ago statement made by one of my aunts to the present. That original statement (saying that people experiencing mental health challenges need to pull up their socks and get back to work) was made over twenty-five years ago. A lot has happened in our lives since then. I need to consciously remind myself that there is no longer any indication she still feels that way and, most likely, her opinions about that subject have changed drastically. Because that statement floored me when she first said it decades ago, I cannot totally forget it, but that may not be fair to her. It's more important to me that I assume her current beliefs on that subject are different than what they used to be—and to not bring those old statements forward into our current relationship.

And then there's me and all the strongly held opinions I confidently espoused decades ago. Nope, that's not me anymore. There may be a relative or long-lost friend out there who may still hold me to some of those opinions and statements, but please know a lot has happened in my life as well, and it has added up to hard-earned wisdom. Funny how life will do that to you.

Part of that wisdom also helps me to know that I can blurt out a retort that sounds like nothing has changed. Chances are that others around me can also unintentionally say or do something closer to their old selves than they'd like. I think of this as accidentally finding that old path down the toboggan hill—even though our true selves wouldn't go there, in a weak moment, an unwelcome blast from the past can slip out.

My daughter and her spouse are really good at handling this and supporting each other through their ongoing desire to grow forward. As a bystander, I notice that if one interrupts or blurts out a snippy retort, they'll notice it, catch themselves, and offer a quick apology for sounding snippy. Wow! I love that. The ideal is to not make mistakes, but perfection is hard to come by. This is a great way to support change in their relationship.

For me, I'm fully aware that I still have much more to learn, so I continue forward, open-minded, and open-hearted to the best of my ability. What about you? Are you leaning in toward making adjustments in what you say and how you say it, demonstrating your open-minded attitude?

Transitions Can Be Hard

Brian "Drew" Chalker's poem "Reason, Season, Lifetime" reminds us that friends can be for a purpose, a lifetime, or for just a few days. In my opinion, each one of these relationships is of value.

I find the same to be true for careers. Among other things, I've been a partner in a start-up technology company, executive director of a (start-up) non-profit, and associate in a workplace mental health organization. Interestingly, I've always been involved at the beginning of each of these. Somehow, I thrive on going all in to get something started. Of course, there's stress associated with that but, for me, it's more stimulating than overwhelming.

However, once there's something operating and in place—something to lose—the stress affects me differently. When I wake in the night, instead of being overstimulated thinking about how to do something, I'm instead panicked about not messing up and ruining it for everyone else.

A close working associate and dear friend of mine once commented that I worry too much about what other people think. In other words (my words), I need to develop a thicker skin and care more about what I believe to be best, rather than worrying about what might upset someone else. While it can be hard to do, that is good advice, and I've thought of it often since then.

This is especially true when you find that your needs and desires change and you, therefore, wish to transition away from one type of work arrangement to something new. This not only applies to work and career, but it can also apply to any other type of relationship, whether it be family, social, or community related.

None of us has a crystal ball. It's pretty natural to have our needs and desires adjust as time goes by, even though we didn't expect it to happen. Is that considered breaking a loyalty, or is it following your destiny? How much does it overlap with the challenge of trying to keep others happy while still following your own desires?

If we shy away from making changes because it feels disloyal (and doesn't meet our need to keep others happy), then we aren't living our right life. And living our right life is probably our most primal need.

As I was standing in line to renew my licence several years ago, I noticed a licence plate frame with the saying:

"Follow Your Heart—Take Your Brain"

I bought it immediately, knowing it was meant for me. Now, whenever I approach my car, I get that short little reminder to go forward toward my dreams—balanced with the reminder that the intelligence and wisdom I've gathered thus far in life will help me to get there.

As I said several sections back, there is no such thing as "no change." Staying still without any change at all is not possible. From a career perspective, the ideal is that we each feel a passion for whatever it is that is taking up our energy. If it continues to be more of the same, because you love what you do, that is perfect! Congrats, you have it all figured out and you are fulfilled as you grow in your role.

However, if your heart is pulling you toward a transition – either an adjustment with your current situation or moving to something brand new – then you need to give that some serious thought. If for no other reason than moving forward in transition will keep you on your toes, leaning forward, with a smile (or look of determination) on your face. Having something to be passionate about stirs our creative juices – and creativity is part of the recipe for resiliency.

Transitions in our career, social, and/or family lives can be challenging, and yes, it takes courage to transition, but it can also be challenging to stay still and not attempt to follow your desires.

You're possibly in the "getting ready to get ready to get ready" stage—and that's a good place to be. If you do lean forward toward following your heart, remember to take your brain.

So Where Is My Cob of Corn?

As you know by now, Louise Hay has been talking to me through her audiotapes / CDs / YouTube videos for many years. In my world, she is the queen of affirmations. Hopefully, you went out and bought her *Experience Your Good Now* book back when I first mentioned it in Section 2. If not, you can find the audio accompaniment on YouTube. Take a listen and see if it appeals to you—maybe it will, and maybe it won't. There are many other speakers and authors that take a different approach to the same concept—there is someone out there for you.

One of her many messages is in relation to doubt. In my words, if you find yourself having a hard time saying positive affirmations because you get a niggling feeling that it's too good to ever be true for you, think of yourself as needing to have a conversation with doubt. Doubt (in the context that Lousie refers to) is the administrative filer of all your thoughts and is located in your gut (or wherever it is in your body where you are most likely to feel that niggling feeling that you're speaking hogwash).

Doubt takes their job very seriously and files all thoughts in carefully tended files. Sometimes, when you send down a thought that's new to you and something you don't typically say, like, "I'm worthy of all of the good things that come into my life," or "I have an abundance of caring and fun-loving friends in my life," doubt may feel it's appropriate to speak up and say that you've made a mistake in saying or thinking that because they haven't heard you say that before and there's no existing file prepared for that thought.

In response to doubt, we may have a tendency to say, "Yes, you're right. How could I have ever believed anything like that, even for a moment?" While undoing your affirmation and changing your thoughts back to unworthiness and no friends might make doubt happy in their administrative role, it isn't doing anything helpful for you.

So instead, Louise Hay tells us to say to doubt, "Thank you for your attention to detail, but I didn't make a mistake. Please start a new file, as there will be many more similar thoughts coming your way."

This visualization and way of thinking appeals to me.

Abraham and Esther Hicks align with this type of thinking when they remind us that when you plant a seed of corn, you don't immediately start asking, "So where's my cob of corn?" Rather, you water and fertilize the ground where you planted the seed, even though you don't yet see any indication of a plant, let alone your cob of corn.

> "We need to tend to the environment and nurture the seedlings (of our hopes and dreams) as we get ready to be ready to be ready to harvest the result."

It's the same with our hopes and dreams. We need to tend to the environment and nurture the seedling as we get ready to be ready to be ready to harvest the corn that results. Change is like that, too. It also needs to be nurtured as we get closer and closer to seeing some type of indication that the change we've been hoping for is actually happening.

When I was zipping down that toboggan hill, desperately hoping to find another way down the hill, I instinctively knew that being kind and compassionate to myself was going to be more effective than hating myself for not being able to do better. Nurturing yourself with non-judgmental loving-kindness is like water, sunshine, fertilizer, and weeding for a corn seed.

Neuroscientist Dr. Davidson backs me up on this. His research team showed that two weeks of compassion and kindness meditation training resulted in changes in brain circuitry. They found these changes were linked to increased positive social behaviours like generosity. See! Brain circuitry and toboggan hills—hard to tell the difference between the two!

That same non-judgmental compassion and kindness will work wonders when you're attempting to support another person who (in your opinion) is stuck in a difficult situation that's going in the wrong direction. Maybe that direction (or that behaviour) is the best they can achieve for themselves at this point in their journey. We're in no position to make that judgment as we don't know all their deep-down thinking and experiences—they possibly don't even know these fully.

Maybe they are in the very preliminary stages of change, and even though they seem to be accomplishing nothing (in our opinion), they are making tiny little adjustments to their way of thinking that are helping them to get ready to get ready to get ready . . . to eventually experience a mindset adjustment that might be somewhat visible to those of us who are on the sidelines.

If you were to bend over that seedling and talk incessantly (even with the best intentions) about what they should be doing to fix their life, maybe you are blocking the sunshine and the rain from reaching them at a time when they need it most. And, in human terms, you're possibly causing them to become even more defensive and obstinate because they just aren't ready yet. And maybe they'll never be ready because we have a different vision for them than what they're meant to have.

Like everything else, there are no guarantees, but letting them know that you support and love them no matter what they choose to do at this point in their journey is more helpful than preaching or difficult arguments about it. You can let them know, by demonstrating it, that you'll be there to listen, to try to understand their perspective, and to ask first if they want your opinion rather than just offering it.

> "Support others by listening, trying to understand their perspective, and asking first if they want your opinion rather than just offering it."

You can also let them know that you have some boundaries/limitations that are important to you and your well-being, such as: I won't answer your phone calls after 10 p.m., I won't go more than once a week to run that errand for you, and I'm not likely to get into conversation with you about politics because we already know we aren't going to agree. Your boundaries will be unique, depending on what you find to be most difficult in your relationship and too much for you to take on. And, of course, your boundaries will adjust and change over time as you discover more about yourself and your relationship.

It's the golden rule—treat others as you wish to be treated. But first, most importantly, be extra sure you are actually treating yourself the way you wish to be treated—with kindness and compassion. Remember that as you plant that little seed of hopefulness within yourself. Nurture your dreams and desires by feeding them loving-kindness and be patient. They'll bloom into what you were hoping for when the time is right.

Getting Past the Challenges

When I started writing this book, one of the few things I knew for sure was that it would be about change—all the many ways that change takes place in our bodies, minds, and behaviours.

Throughout, I have made references several times to reframing a difficult thought or situation into a better or more promising way of thinking about it. My therapist was a huge help in getting me started on this path by gently nudging me away from long-held critical thoughts toward kinder and more promising thoughts.

If a visual helps, then think of it from the perspective of focussing on a dog. Are you looking at (talking about) his cute little face? Or are you focussed on his rear end? Disgusting doggy rear-end stories may be humorous now and then, but is that really what you want the majority of your conversations to be about? Turn that puppy around and get a better look at his cute little face—tell that tale.

Hopefully, we can now hear when we are in the midst of dramatizing and retelling a troublesome story just for the sake of conversation or entertainment. Each time we notice ourselves going to the negative in our speech, we can be sure that our thoughts were already there—and they will continue to stay in the negative until we decide to either reframe the situation (looking for the positives) or drop the story altogether.

> "When you change the way you look at things, the things you look at change."
>
> WAYNE DYER

Norman Doidge, in his book *Brain Bliss*, and other researchers, have studied our brains and discovered that the more focus we put on something, the stronger it becomes and the more it grows up there in our grey matter. That is true, in particular, when we switch it up and work on our ability to be in the moment (be mindful), practice gratitude, and/or meditate. (Remember those lists of resiliency-building practices?)

We can lean forward into these bigger concepts by doing simple little tactics like nurturing micro-moments of positivity or taking a moment to ground ourselves when in the middle of a busy day. Taking the time to sit down with a journal or listen to a guided meditation is great, but don't put it all off until you have the time or inclination to do it "properly." Remember that good enough is the goal; waiting for the perfect opportunity will likely result in a very long wait. Pick up a few quick and easy habits now that appeal to you, the kind of habits that you can squeeze into your day, like when you're riding an elevator or waiting at a stop light.

Above all else, try to notice your inner voice, as well as what you say out loud. Just notice it. Please don't be angry or frustrated by it; just notice it—and then give yourself some understanding and kindness.

If your inner voice is mad or sad or mean, then for sure you could use some loving-kindness and remind yourself, "You're getting better every day at noticing your thoughts and re-languageing them into kind, calm words." And you may need to have a word with doubt and give the reminder that this way of thinking and speaking is new, so open that new folder and start filing!

My go-to is to get into YouTube and listen to one of my favourite authors/speakers. The other morning, I was listening to Abraham Hicks, and they were telling one of their stories about Esther towing a car behind the big "Monster Bus." They realized when they got to their destination that the brakes of the car had been on the whole way—yet with the power of their big bus, they couldn't feel the drag of the braked car while they were on the road.

It made me realize that perfection in our inner thoughts and outer behaviour doesn't need to be our goal. As long as we have enough steam (leaning forward enough) with our thoughts and language, being even a little more positive than the week before, the impact of some of the negatives will be less. One or two difficult thoughts can be difficult in the moment and temporarily put on the brakes, but if we strive to think about all of the positives that are up there in the front of the bus, it's going to be okay.

The next time you get stuck or feeling hopeless because the negative stuff has arisen *again*, try thinking about getting back up on the hay wagon—or leaning forward toward the front of the bus—and *know* that you are getting better day by day, week by week, at leaning forward, to the point that much of the time you don't even notice that the brakes are on in that little car you're towing along behind.

It's All Gonna Be Okay

"When the student is ready the teacher will appear."

TAO TE CHING

I am very aware that the yoga teacher who led that six-week community yoga class was the perfect person to introduce me to the aspects of yoga that were most useful to me.

I am very aware that my psychotherapist was the perfect person for me to spend five years of my life with. He had the intelligence, gentle kindness, and quiet reframing that allowed me cultural permission to be the kind of person who did therapy, and he helped me explore thoughts that might have been laced with too much guilt if I'd thought them on my own. Plus . . . he was willing to be flexible and respect my preferences. (No couch for me!!)

I am very aware that Denise was the perfect friend for me at a time when I was ready to start the path of inner exploration and to experiment with feeling that it was okay to *do* less and *be* more. If she had shown up years earlier, I could <u>never</u> have spent so much time "trying" to be unproductive and to calm life down. But the time was right and, thankfully, she was there ready to laugh or listen—whichever was called for.

And, I am also very aware that picking up the *Don't Sweat the Small Stuff* book was the right book at the right time.

There are a zillion other examples of the right person, book, or resource showing up when I, the student, was ready for that phase of learning.

Hopefully, you've found this book at the right time for you. Hopefully, it has sparked your thinking in the manner that is best suited for you. You may not be finding yourself uncontrollably slipping down toboggan hills, looking for a turnoff from the inevitable disappointment in yourself, but I hope that my visual spurs you toward your own visual and the concept that works for you.

I have faith we'll all find our way toward being the people we were meant to be. I'm feeling happy, proud of myself, and content (for the most part) at this point in my life. I love knowing that you will be as well. ♥♥☺☺

ABOUT THE AUTHOR

Kim Sunderland is co-author of the Mental Health Commission of Canada's Peer Support Guidelines. She was the inaugural Executive Director of the national non-profit Peer Support Canada and was co-chair of the 2014 and 2016 National Conferences on Peer Support in Halifax and Toronto.

She has lived and taught the tenets of *It's All Gonna Be Okay* as a workshop facilitator and peer support leader in communities and workplaces. In addition, she has supported others—friends, family, and peers—using these same stories and strategies.

Kim lives in Mississauga, Ontario, with her husband, Terry, and a short drive from each of her three adult children.

www.ingramcontent.com/pod-product-compliance
Lightning Source LLC
LaVergne TN
LVHW090942210125
801725LV00001B/74